How RTI Works in

SECONDARY SCHOOLS

Evelyn S. Johnson
Lori Smith
Monica L. Harris

FOREWORD BY
Daryl F. Mellard

CORWIN
A SAGE Company

For information:

Corwin
A SAGE Company
2455 Teller Road
Thousand Oaks, California 91320
(800) 233-9936
Fax: (800) 417-2466
www.corwinpress.com

SAGE Ltd.
1 Oliver's Yard
55 City Road
London EC1Y 1SP
United Kingdom

SAGE Pvt. Ltd.
B 1/I 1 Mohan Cooperative
   Industrial Area
Mathura Road, New Delhi 110 044
India

SAGE Asia-Pacific Pte. Ltd.
33 Pekin Street #02-01
Far East Square
Singapore 048763

Printed in the United States of America

Library of Congress Cataloging-in-Publication Data

Johnson, Evelyn S., 1969-
How RTI works in secondary schools/Evelyn S. Johnson, Lori Smith, Monica L. Harris.
    p. cm.
Includes bibliographical references and index.
ISBN 978-1-4129-7099-0 (cloth)
ISBN 978-1-4129-7100-3 (pbk.)

   1. Remedial teaching—United States. 2. Education, Secondary—United States. 3. School failure—United States—Prevention. 4. School improvement programs—United States. I. Smith, Lori, 1969- II. Harris, Monica L. III. Title.

LB1029.R4J64 2009
371.3—dc22   2009026650

This book is printed on acid-free paper.

11   12   13   14   15   10   9   8   7   6   5   4   3

Acquisitions Editor:	David Chao
Editorial Assistant:	Sarah Bartlett
Production Editor:	Veronica Stapleton
Copy Editor:	Amy Rosenstein
Typesetter:	C&M Digitals (P) Ltd.
Proofreader:	Dennis W. Webb
Indexer:	Molly Hall
Cover Designer:	Rose Storey
Graphic Designer:	Scott Van Atta

How
RTI
Works in
SECONDARY SCHOOLS

Contents

Foreword

Response to Intervention (RTI) is a national education initiative for providing services to all students and improving identification of students with learning disabilities. Many states and districts are viewing RTI as an important framework for aligning many of their school improvement initiatives. Given the potential of an RTI framework to result in improved student learning outcomes, one might anticipate much interest in implementing RTI as a means for school improvement. RTI can be an effective but complex initiative to implement well. To implement RTI successfully, a number of essential components are required. Essential components within an RTI framework include the careful coordination of instruction, intervention, and assessment procedures, to include scientifically supported practice and high-quality instruction in general education classrooms.

School staffs face multiple challenges in implementing RTI, and these challenges can be exacerbated at the secondary level. One critical task is implementing the specific tools of RTI—student assessment and interventions. Although the tools are important, implementation of RTI will only work when school staff also integrate RTI as part of their vision for educating students and for their roles and responsibilities as professionals. As part of that process, RTI requires changes in the interaction among administrators, teachers, parents, and other professional staff. Another significant challenge of RTI is integrating the approach into the existing structure of a school. When a student is struggling with learning, RTI can provide a system to support a student by first ensuring that the general education instruction includes the use of evidence-based practice, that all students are screened for academic difficulties, and that research-based interventions are available to students who require additional support.

The implementation literature is rife with examples of education initiatives that are not successfully implemented on a large scale. A growing body of literature supports the strong role that shared vision and common understandings play in successful implementation efforts. For example, in an RTI model site study conducted by the National Research Center on Learning Disabilities (NRCLD), strong administrative leadership and a commitment to ongoing professional development were two of the most consistently found features of sites with successful RTI models. Conversely, challenges that were noted across sites included ensuring that staff members understand their role and responsibilities and that they work out the "chemistry" or needed interaction patterns to make the system work effectively.

With RTI, schools identify students at risk for poor learning outcomes, monitor student progress, provide evidence-based interventions, and adjust the intensity and nature of those interventions depending on a student's responsiveness. The fundamental issue at the secondary level is the quality of the primary level of curriculum and instructional practices. Some critical questions that can be addressed through the use of an RTI framework in the context of school reform include determining what happens for students whose performance is well below grade level, what strategies are in place to ensure that students will get the critical content, and whether procedures for teaching powerful learning strategies are embedded in courses across the curriculum. Strong school leadership will be critical to answering these questions and coordinating the staffs' efforts and talents.

The necessary conditions for ensuring successful RTI implementation include sustained investments in professional development programs; engaged administrators who set expectations for adoption and proper implementation; district-level support to encourage staff to embrace the principles of RTI and develop the requisite skills; and, finally, developing a willingness to stay the course. The essential point is that rigorous implementation will have to be a core focus of the school's agenda. To successfully bring about change, schools will need to address the forces at play, including not only understanding the specifics of the new framework, but also redefining roles and being provided sufficient time to make sense of the changes required under RTI. In other words, the combination of skill development coupled with new understandings of roles, responsibilities, and shared vision is what will support schools' successful RTI implementation.

In their text, Johnson, Smith, and Harris cogently capture this combination of tasks: explaining the specifics of the RTI and the RTI implementation process within the larger context of school functioning. In addition, the authors' integration of RTI with other existing frameworks, such as Professional Learning Communities (PLC), Data-based Decision Making, and Positive Behavior Intervention and Support, present helpful strategies of supporting schools in their "sense-making" endeavors for RTI implementation. By drawing on specific examples of RTI implementation at the middle and high school levels, the authors have provided a powerful means of demonstrating the components in practice. In short, practitioners will find this text an extremely useful resource as they begin their implementation process.

Daryl F. Mellard, PhD

Acknowledgments

This work would not have been possible without significant contributions from many professionals in the field, including the school staffs from Cheyenne Mountain Junior High in Colorado Springs, Colorado; Moscow Junior and Senior High Schools in Moscow, Idaho; Coopersville Middle School in Coopersville, Michigan; Mattawan High School in Mattawan, Michigan; and Chisago Lakes High School in Lindstrom, Minnesota. Finally, we acknowledge the editorial work of Julie Tollefson, whose talents as an editor significantly enhanced the readability of this text.

Corwin wishes to acknowledge the following peer reviewers for their editorial insight and guidance.

Frederick Brigham
Associate Professor of Special Education
George Mason University
Fairfax, Virginia

Eugene Edgar
Professor, College of Education
University of Washington
Seattle, Washington

Kimberly Kysar
Speech-Language Pathologist and RTI Coordinator
Yukon Public Schools, Central Elementary
Yukon, Oklahoma

Ryan Pfahler
Middle School Principal
Coopersville Area Public Schools
Coopersville, Michigan

Nicole Power
RTI Coordinator and Speech Language Pathologist
Bethany Public Schools
Bethany, Oklahoma

Nancy Thomas Price
RTI Coordinator
Idaho State Department of Education
Boise, Idaho

Holly Windram
Assistant Director of Special Education
St. Croix River Education District
Rush City, Minnesota

About the Authors

Evelyn S. Johnson, EdD, is an Associate Professor of Special Education at Boise State University (BSU) and the coauthor of *RTI: A Practitioner's Guide to Implementing Response to Intervention.* She began her career in Washington in 1994 as a special education teacher, and then at the University of Washington, Seattle, where her research focused on the inclusion of students with disabilities in accountability systems. Dr. Johnson's work on assessment for students with disabilities has included research on accommodations and alternate assessments as well as research on screening for reading problems. Prior to joining the faculty at BSU, she worked as a research associate for the National Research Center on Learning Disabilities (NRCLD), where she developed numerous technical assistance products to assist state and local educational agencies on RTI and learning disability identification–related issues. Currently, her research focuses on RTI implementation at the secondary levels.

Lori Smith, PhD, is principal at Cheyenne Mountain Junior High in Colorado Springs, Colorado. She has served in public education for fifteen years, nine of which have been in school administration. She began her career as a high school biology and chemistry teacher in 1994 in Colorado. Her work and systematic implementation of RTI at Cheyenne Mountain has led to several state-level presentations, publications, and consultations on RTI implementation. Ms. Smith's commitment to action research on RTI at the secondary level was inspired by the support of Dr. Evelyn Johnson while completing her doctoral degree in Education Leadership and Administration.

 **Monica L. Harris, PhD,** is an Assistant Professor at Grand Valley State University (GVSU) in the College of Education. She began her career in education at the secondary level and has experience teaching adolescents in general and special education settings as well as developing and implementing programs for students who struggle academically or who are at risk for school failure. Prior to joining the faculty at GVSU, she received her doctoral degree in Special Education from the University of Kansas, where her research focused on strategy instruction and adolescent literacy. Dr. Harris is part of the Strategic Instruction Model (SIM) Professional Developer's Network and works with school districts to implement tiered intervention using research-based instructional strategies. Currently, her research interests include developing instructional strategies for use in academically diverse classrooms, teacher preparation, and collaborative teaching models.

1

What Is RTI?

Response to Intervention, or RTI, is a multitiered approach to providing instruction and targeted intervention to improve student outcomes. Although there are variations on the number of tiers included in RTI models, RTI is most often conceptualized as a three-tiered system (see Figure 1.1), in which Tier 1 represents the general education instruction, Tier 2 represents a secondary level of intervention for students who require additional supports to be successful, and Tier 3 represents special education. RTI has roots in the preventive sciences, with its reliance on a population-based, proactive approach to ensuring strong educational experiences for all students. It is estimated that with this emphasis on providing high-quality, research-based instruction to the general population, approximately eighty percent of students will achieve targeted outcomes with general education instruction alone. However, even with a strong general education program in place, a small percentage of students, approximately fifteen percent, will require more intense interventions to make adequate academic progress. RTI relies on a system of early identification to determine which students will require this level of intensity. Finally, for approximately five percent of the population, tertiary intervention (or special education) will be needed for students to make progress toward alternate performance benchmarks and high school completion requirements. As Figure 1.1 demonstrates, all students should participate in and access the Tier 1 program in some way. For some students, that may require the additional support of an intervention (Tier 2), or it may require specially designed instruction (Tier 3) that provides access to the general education curriculum.

Figure 1.1   A Tiered Model of Service Delivery

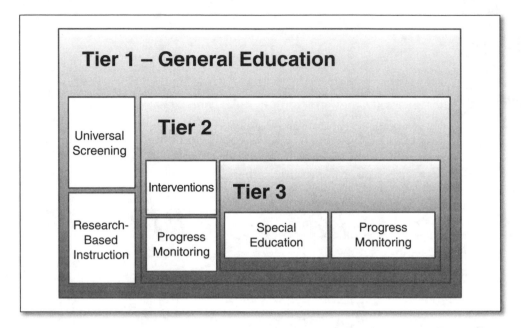

PURPOSE OF RTI AT THE SECONDARY LEVEL

RTI is a schoolwide initiative that has as its ultimate goal school improvement across the K–12 grade-level spectrum. At the elementary level, RTI models have been described as having three primary purposes: (a) screening and prevention of academic skill deficits primarily related to reading and mathematics, (b) early identification and intervention for students at risk for developing learning problems, and (c) learning disability determination (Mellard & Johnson, 2008). The primary goal is to identify early those students at risk for not developing the foundation of academic skills that will enable them to become successful and independent learners as they progress through the K–12 system. With this system in place, the expectation is that all students will exit the elementary setting ready to meet the challenges of the more demanding content at junior high and, finally, to develop and learn in high school the skills and knowledge that will enable them to be successful once they leave high school.

Although RTI at the elementary school level is designed to help individual students develop the capacity to read, write, and perform mathematics at a level that will enable them to be successful in a secondary setting, not all students will meet this rigorous standard. Students who enter secondary schools without strong basic academic skills are at risk for learning problems across numerous content areas as their teachers require them to read and write to learn content. An increasing number of students enter secondary schools ill-prepared to meet the demands of a challenging junior and senior high curriculum (Jerald, 2006). Many biology, history, health, and economics teachers find their traditional approach to teaching is not effective in meeting the needs of many of their students.

In addition to the changing demands in content, once students enter the secondary grades, they encounter noticeable structural changes in the school setting. First, they no longer have one classroom teacher who teaches "ninth grade" the way an elementary teacher teaches "third grade." Teachers at the secondary level focus on content (e.g., "I'm a history teacher" or "I teach biology"). Most junior and senior high schools do not teach students how to read but rather use reading and writing as the primary means through which teaching and learning occur. Finally, the goals and outcomes at secondary levels are quite different from those at elementary levels. Whereas elementary schools prepare students to develop skills to be successful in later school years, what is the goal of secondary schools? Not all students will have the same long-term goals. For example, some students will attend a four-year college or university. Others will seek vocational or technical training. Others may attend a local community college to continue preparation for a four-year institution of higher learning. Still others will immediately join the workforce or armed services.

Though long-term goals may vary, for all students, obtaining a high school diploma is a shared short-term outcome. Without a high school diploma, students have very little chance of being successful later in life. Indeed, research indicates that high school dropouts face significantly higher probabilities of incarceration, poverty, and need for social services (Schweinhart, 2004). Although districts and states differ on the specifics of high school graduation requirements, most include a combination of successful course and credit completion, successful performance on exit exams, and other requirements such as senior projects. As an increasing number of states require successful completion of exit exams to receive a high school diploma, performance on these assessments, along with other graduation requirements such as senior projects and credit attainment, help provide a common system of evaluation for all students.

In summary, as depicted in Figure 1.2, the purposes of RTI at the secondary level are similar to but distinct from the purposes at the elementary level. The primary purpose of RTI at the secondary level is to build the capacity of the school to meet the increasing demands for a diverse student population to meet rigorous standards for graduation. A secondary purpose is to ensure appropriate instruction and intervention is provided to all students. A final purpose is to provide a system that will support continuous school improvement to improve outcomes for all students.

Figure 1.2 Purposes of RTI at Different Levels

Purposes of RTI at the Elementary Level		Purposes of RTI at the Secondary Level	
Screening and Prevention	• Identifies students as "at risk" and provides early intervention	Build Capacity	• Schools can meet the demands of a diverse student population
Early Intervention	• Enhances the general curriculum for all students and provides intervention and remediation	Intervention	• Support students at risk for dropping out of school
Disability Determination	• Determines a student's response to instruction and intervention as one part of disability determination	Continuous School Improvement	• Better teaching and learning through an integrated system

HOW RTI WORKS

Tiered System of Instruction and Intervention

A strong general education program is the foundation for a successful RTI program. At the secondary level (grades 6–12), one of the most positive potential outcomes of RTI implementation is the provision of a systematic process through which schools can improve their general education instruction. Integrating the use of evidence-based practices that meet the needs of a diverse population of students across the content areas is the fundamental requirement for a successful Tier 1 (or general education) component.

Even with strong general education instruction, some students will require additional support to be successful in the general education program. This level of support is provided in Tier 2. In Tier 2, interventions that focus on specific, targeted skills are provided for students who struggle with the Tier 1 curriculum. These include academic, behavior, and engagement skills delivered through either a *standard protocol approach* or a *problem-solving approach* (these approaches are further explained in Chapter 6). For example, students who have difficulties in reading may require interventions that support their reading development. In addition to receiving these interventions, they also may require accommodations in the content area (e.g., science) classroom, such as graphic organizers or alternate presentation formats. A layered approach that provides targeted skill instruction as well as accommodations has been demonstrated to be very effective in supporting struggling students (Swanson & Deshler, 2003).

Finally, although many students with disabilities can have many of their needs met through accommodations in the general education class and the support of Tier 2, special education services will be required for a small percentage of students. In this text, we define Tier 3 as special education. In some cases, special education may consist of more intense interventions than those provided in Tier 2. In other cases, special education may consist of alternate performance benchmarks, curriculum, and instruction.

Integrated Assessment and Instruction System

High-quality, research-based general education instruction and targeted interventions that increase in intensity depending on student need are the hallmarks of an effective RTI system. RTI is also characterized by the integration of the instructional system with an assessment system that accomplishes many things, to include the following:

1. The system screens *all* students to determine who may be at risk for poor academic outcomes.

2. It monitors student progress at all tiers.

3. It integrates a diagnostic procedure for students who are at risk to determine the nature and extent of their learning problems and to determine appropriate courses of action.

4. It provides program- and school-level data that may serve as the basis for making decisions about continuous school improvement efforts.

A Systemic Approach

Although we discuss the components of RTI throughout this text, RTI is not simply a number of components implemented in a disjointed fashion. If a school has all of the required components but lacks the integrated system that makes the components work, RTI will not be successful. For example, early reports on RTI implementation at the secondary level indicate that some schools adopted an intervention program that targeted reading but then failed to make changes in the schedule and to connect the intervention to the general education program (Vaughn, Speece, & Linan-Thompson, 2008). In addition, the general education curriculum was not examined to determine how struggling readers could make progress in the content-area courses. Finally, placement in the intervention was driven by administrative factors (e.g., scheduling) rather than by Data-based Decision Making (DBDM). The result is a haphazard approach to RTI that does not promote strong student achievement.

For RTI to be effective, a school must not only put the necessary components into place, but must also integrate the components to become an effective system. To make that happen, leadership at all levels will be the linchpin for success. At the national level, for example, strong and coordinated technical assistance from research and technical assistance centers is needed to provide guidance on best practices that inform implementation. At the time of this writing, such assistance is emerging in full force (see the Resources section at the end of this text for more information).

At the state level, policies that support implementation and professional development for RTI are imperative. States that have strong, concise guidance documents that communicate a cohesive message about the purpose of RTI can effectively guide implementation efforts and support school districts. The development of policy is only the initial step, however. The states' responsibility in making RTI work is to develop a comprehensive system of professional development and to coordinate policies and procedures across many areas, such as curriculum, instruction, special education, English language learner programs, and assessment.

Districts have the responsibility of aligning RTI efforts across the K–12 level by developing policies and supports for building-level implementation. Finally, at the school level, building leaders will need to coordinate the many moving parts and guide school staff through a large culture shift. For these reasons, we believe that in addition to providing the specifics about the process of RTI and its individual components, a strong focus on describing the leader responsibilities will better support secondary schools as they implement RTI. In this text, we focus on the leader requirements for implementation at the school level. Although we do not discuss state and district policy in detail, district-level and state-level leaders will also benefit from a more thorough understanding of the implementation process.

RTI as School Improvement

As described in this text, RTI is a comprehensive model for school improvement, encompassing nearly every aspect of school function. Because RTI is comprehensive in scope, schools may feel overwhelmed when beginning with RTI implementation. Implementing reform and system changes, especially in secondary schools, is a significant undertaking that requires strong leadership, a commitment from involved stakeholders and participants, and the acknowledgement that implementing change is a multiyear process (Fullan, 2004). In addition, RTI is just one of many recent policy initiatives that compete for a school's resources (Mellard & Johnson, 2008). Schools are faced with an increasing number of policy initiatives, each targeting a specific population, or a specific aspect of school function, that often do not include information on how the particular initiative fits within the larger context of school functioning. When a policy initiative is interpreted on its own, as if its practices are unrelated to others, the result can be a fragmented, haphazard approach to school improvement that rarely has staying power (Spillane, Reiser, & Reimer, 2002). Instead, policy initiatives should be considered within the context of the school system, aligned with the school vision and mission and integrated to obtain stated school goals.

In this section, we briefly outline three current reform frameworks—Professional Learning Communities (PLC: DuFour & Eaker, 1998), Positive Behavior Intervention and Support (PBIS: Sugai & Horner, 1999), and Data-based Decision Making (DBDM: American Association of School Administrators [AASA], 2002)—that can work in conjunction with the RTI framework to effectively and efficiently guide school improvement efforts. Numerous other policy initiatives can also be aligned within an RTI framework. We focus on PLCs, PBIS, and DBDM because they have been successfully integrated within RTI models at the secondary schools profiled throughout this book. An in-depth description of these frameworks is beyond the scope of this text, but the Resources section of this text directs the interested reader to further, helpful guidance.

HOW RTI FITS WITH OTHER EDUCATION INITIATIVES

RTI and the PLC Framework

RTI integrates best practices in instruction, intervention, and assessment to promote better student outcomes. Currently, these best practices are much better understood, defined, and available for the early elementary grades. At the secondary level, many of the building blocks for implementing a successful secondary RTI process are available but are not as well defined and require a more concerted effort for implementation. A good starting point to lead this effort for RTI implementation is the PLC framework.

PLCs, as described by DuFour and Eaker (1998), are collaborative groups of professionals who (a) work to analyze and identify problems, (b) devise solutions, (c) determine the effect of enacting solutions, and (d) make adjustments as needed. Comprising practitioners working together to solve problems and make improvements in practice, a PLC is in a unique position to address not only the technical aspects of solving a problem (e.g., What instructional strategies best meet the needs of English language learners in our school?), but also the social aspects (e.g., How do we consider the values of our community members when implementing this change?). When major reform efforts are implemented in such a way that both the technical and the social context are addressed, the result is sustainable improvement (Reid, 2007). PLCs allow schools to interpret and make sense of reform efforts, avoiding the problem of treating systemic changes merely as technical problems (Heifetz & Linsky, 2002) and instead discussing how best to apply new approaches within existing school cultures.

PLCs support the implementation of RTI in two primary ways:

1. They allow the school leader to delegate specific tasks, such as investigating new instructional practices. Involving school staff helps gain school buy-in and ownership of school practice.

2. They allow a school to begin with one essential component for implementation, laying the foundation for continuing the process as other elements of the RTI process are brought to scale.

Many of the structures required for PLCs are likely in place at the secondary school. For example, departments may already collaborate for curriculum mapping or other activities. These meeting times may be refocused to include other important components of RTI such as screening, intervention, and progress-monitoring procedures. In subsequent chapters of this text, we provide descriptions of these components and detailed guidance to direct their implementation. Organizing PLCs around these components can serve as a helpful system for RTI implementation. For example, see the textbox "RTI and PLCs in Practice" for a description of how one junior high used the two frameworks for successful RTI implementation.

Textbox 1.1   RTI and PLCs in Practice

The PLC framework was used as the primary vehicle for RTI implementation at Cheyenne Mountain Junior High School. When the school began the process, the principal designated several PLC teams:

1. A "core" RTI team, responsible for reviewing student information and making decisions about which students would require academic interventions.

2. A "Tier 1" team, responsible for researching, educating, and evaluating instructional strategies for use across the Tier 1 program to improve student learning.

3. A "PBIS" team, responsible for reviewing student information and making decisions about which students would require behavioral interventions.

4. An "intervention" team, responsible for researching and developing a bank of intervention strategies based on student need at Cheyenne Mountain. After year two of implementation, the PBIS and intervention teams were combined into one intervention team that focused on both academics and behavior.

5. An "assessment" team, responsible for developing screening and progress-monitoring procedures integrated with the instruction and intervention at Tiers 1 and 2.

The principal provided the necessary administrative support to enable the teams to function effectively. For example, she designated routine meeting times and adjusted the schedule to ensure that the PLC teams had adequate time and facilities for meeting. She also scheduled staff training on the PLC framework and the RTI process. Through the integration of these initiatives, the entire staff has ownership of the RTI process, and there is a much greater integration of the process across grade levels and content areas as a result of increased collaboration and professional development.

RTI and PBIS

In this text, we include PBIS under the umbrella of RTI. In other words, as described in this book, RTI encompasses *both* academics and behavior. The school models that are profiled throughout this book have integrated academics and behavior because they recognize that many students present with a combination of issues, and schools must work to provide interventions that support both the academic and behavioral needs of their students. Research and practice clearly demonstrate that, oftentimes, both learning and behavioral problems contribute to academic difficulties (Kennelly & Monrad, 2007), and this is particularly the case by the time students enter secondary schools (Kennelly & Monrad, 2007). At the secondary level, therefore, efforts to intervene for learning problems will generally be more effective when behavioral issues also are considered.

A model for addressing discipline and behavioral concerns that shares with RTI both the philosophical underpinnings of a prevention approach and a tiered system for implementation is PBIS (Sugai & Horner, 1999). Like RTI, PBIS is a tiered model of service delivery that stems from the prevention sciences to take a proactive approach to improving schoolwide behavior and discipline. Like RTI, PBIS begins with a schoolwide focus to establish clear and consistent expectations for behavior, with well-defined consequences. It is a positive approach to creating a school climate free from behavioral problems. Like RTI, PBIS recognizes that even when this proactive approach is implemented, a small percentage of students may require some more intensive support to establish positive behavior, and an even smaller percentage of students may require specially designed services or special education to assist in the management and development of positive behavior.

RTI and PBIS share many common features, including screening, differentiated instruction, progress monitoring, and interventions targeted to support student needs (Sandomierski, Kincaid, & Algozzine, 2007). Emerging data on effective implementation of an RTI model that includes both academics and behavior (e.g., Johnson & Smith, 2008; Windram, Scierka, & Silberglitt, 2007) are promising. Descriptions of these models in practice are provided throughout the text and in greater detail in Chapter 8.

RTI and DBDM

A recent focus in school improvement efforts has been the use of data to inform decision making at all levels. DBDM requires schools and districts to collect, analyze, report, evaluate, and communicate through data (AASA, 2002). DBDM can help measure student progress, measure program effectiveness, meet federal and state reporting requirements, show trends in performance, and maintain the focus on improvement efforts (AASA, 2002). Like other school-improvement frameworks, DBDM involves not only building the technical capacity to collect and evaluate data but also a paradigm shift for many stakeholders. The Council of Chief State School Officers (CCSSO) developed the following guidelines for implementing DBDM:

1. Establish a school improvement team.

2. Develop a hypothesis.

3. Gather data to assess needs.

4. Evaluate and use the data.

5. Develop a data-based plan of action.

6. Monitor progress and document success.

With the focus on data, DBDM approaches to school improvement are consistent with the RTI and PBIS frameworks. With the focus on collaborative problem solving, DBDM also is consistent with the PLC model. RTI includes collecting assessment data through screening, progress-monitoring tools, and outcome measures. These data are analyzed at the individual student level to make specific decisions about student progress. At the classroom and grade levels, data analysis also informs general decisions about instruction, and at the school level it informs decisions about curriculum, instruction, and program effectiveness.

As described here, the original focus of RTI as an early identification and prevention model is greatly expanded to include continuous school improvement, especially when it is implemented to include PLC, PBIS, and DBDM. In Figure 1.3, we've depicted an expanded conceptualization of RTI that brings together numerous research-based practices and frameworks to lead to continuous school improvement. In the subsequent chapters of this text, we describe these research-based practices in detail and provide resources that will support their implementation. In Chapter 8, we revisit this figure to provide an overall summary of the RTI process.

Figure 1.3   An Integrated Model of RTI

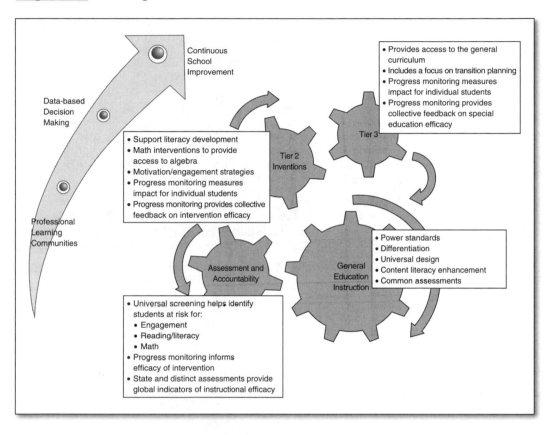

PURPOSE OF THIS BOOK

The purpose of this book is to provide information, resources, and guidance on the implementation of RTI at the secondary level (grades 6–12). A growing number of resources related to RTI are available, but much of the literature and research to date are targeted toward the elementary grades and, more specifically, to reading. Yet, many states across the country envision RTI as a K–12 model, despite little guidance on how to use RTI at the secondary level. Our goal in writing this book is to provide initial guidance as secondary schools begin the process of implementation. As RTI implementation continues to scale up across the nation, the research base will expand and provide further guidance on improving the RTI process. As a starting point, we draw on existing school-based RTI models as well as the current research base on effective practices in secondary level education to identify current best practices for key components of RTI and to offer specific guidance to building leaders for making the process a success.

HOW THIS BOOK IS ORGANIZED

This book is organized in four main sections: (a) an overview that consists of a description of RTI, its purpose at the secondary level, and challenges specific to the secondary level in its implementation (Chapter 1); (b) an implementation and evaluation guide that provides information on getting started and evaluating the process and the outcomes of implementation (Chapter 2); (c) leader perspectives on RTI implementation (Chapter 3); (d) detailed descriptions and guides to implementation for each of the components of an RTI model (Chapters 4–7); and (e) a concluding summary about the future of RTI along with case story descriptions of two models of implementation (Chapter 8).

Within each section we have provided "in practice" examples from actual RTI models in place in schools today as well as a "leader check" for implementation. The implementation checklist from *RTI: A Practitioner's Guide to Implementing Response to Intervention* (Mellard & Johnson, 2008) is included in the Appendix. In addition, this text provides a list of web-based resources to assist practitioners as they move forward with RTI implementation.

SUMMARY

School improvement is a continuous effort that cannot be accomplished without a strong commitment from all involved (Gersten, Chard, & Baker, 2000). As a process of school improvement, RTI requires the same strong commitment. In 2003, the National Research Center on Learning Disabilities conducted a national model RTI site identification project (Mellard, Byrd, Johnson, Tellefson, & Boesche, 2004). The purpose of this project was to identify schools that had effectively and successfully implemented RTI. As a part of this effort, nineteen sites were identified nationally. These sites had implemented RTI differently but shared the following characteristics that contributed to their success:

1. They recognized that successful implementation was a multiple-year commitment.

2. They began implementation with a component already nearly in place, then continued with subsequent components.

3. They integrated professional development and collaboration as the primary means for capacity building and sustainability. (Mellard & Johnson, 2008)

Taken together, these characteristics remind us that the key to successful RTI implementation will be a collaborative effort spearheaded by strong leadership that can integrate and align the many moving parts of the system.

RTI is a comprehensive framework that encompasses numerous facets of school functioning. At the secondary level, a primary purpose of RTI is to build the capacity of the school to meet the needs of an increasingly diverse student population. As described in this book, numerous existing policies are subsumed under the RTI framework to drive school-improvement efforts. These include the PLC, PBIS, and DBDM frameworks. When schools are able to integrate RTI with other existing frameworks and recognize that implementation is a multiple-year investment, they are more likely to be successful with RTI implementation. In the remaining chapters of this book, we discuss the unique challenges of RTI implementation in secondary schools and provide guidance for implementation of RTI components, drawing from school-based examples to facilitate understanding of the process.

2

Implementation and Continuous Improvement

OVERVIEW

Congratulations! You have committed to beginning the process of RTI implementation. You now probably have three important questions:

1. How and where do you start?

2. How will you know if you are proceeding in a manner supportive of successful implementation?

3. How do you know whether your efforts are successful?

This is the order in which many practitioners will ask these questions. In this chapter, however, we offer a process for implementation and continuous improvement that draws on the use of a backwards planning approach (Wiggins & McTighe, 2007). The goal is to provide a process through which schools can assess the integrity of RTI implementation—that is, are we implementing it in the way in which it was intended? Answering this question then leads to identifying and prioritizing areas of concern so that schools can work toward continuous improvement.

In a backwards planning approach, the first question a school should ask is "How do we define success?" and then align all that it does to this desired end state. Essential steps in backwards planning include the following:

1. Identifying the desired outcomes.

2. Articulating how RTI is expected to lead to these outcomes.

3. Listing the events and actions necessary if RTI is to achieve these outcomes and work as expected.

4. Determining sources of data that will be key to making informed decisions regarding both the process of establishing an RTI model and the attainment of the desired outcomes.

5. Developing a system for analyzing and evaluating that data.

6. Providing a mechanism through which adjustments and improvements to the RTI process can be made. (Worthen, Sanders, & Fitzpatrick, 1997)

Through this process, schools are able to maintain a "relentless focus on the long-term mission of the school" (Wiggins & McTighe, 2007). This focus can prevent RTI from becoming just one more school reform initiative that falls prey to the "Attempt—Attack—Abandon" cycle (Deshler & Mellard, 2006) in which a school attempts to launch an innovative program, but before the program can be evaluated or revised, it is attacked for being too cumbersome or ineffective, leading the school to abandon the program in favor of the next new promising alternative.

Once the desired outcomes are stated, the school can work through the remaining steps to begin the process of implementation and continuous improvement. Each of the steps in this process is explained below.

WHAT ARE THE DESIRED OUTCOMES?

The first step in the planning process involves stating the desired outcomes. Put another way, what does the school hope to accomplish through its implementation of RTI? Identifying the outcomes a school hopes to achieve is an important strategy for assessing the success of any initiative. Before a school begins to develop an RTI model, it needs to state and define its desired outcomes. For most schools, we assume that the desired outcomes will focus on improved teaching and learning, and that those outcomes are reflected in the school's mission statement. Although the focus of school goals may vary somewhat, the goals that are consistently associated with successful reform efforts have embraced personal, social, vocational, and academic attributes (Goodlad, Mantle-Bromley, & Goodlad, 2004). Thus, schools should identify the goals and values associated with these four dimensions as their first step in the evaluation process. Many schools will have clear statements about high academic achievement, but what goals do they have for students in terms of personal, social, and vocational attributes?

Revisiting (or developing) your school's mission statement prior to beginning the process of RTI implementation greatly assists in the alignment of the process with your school's goals. To help with this activity, use the sample worksheet in Figure 2.1 to write down your mission statement, and elaborate what the mission statement means for each of the four dimensions (personal, social, vocational, and academic attributes). A small team might develop a draft of these school goals, and then distribute the draft to other building faculty and staff for review. Once staff members reach consensus on desired outcomes, the resulting document becomes the school's "simplification system" (Honig & Hatch, 2004) for guiding activities and evaluating how the RTI processes adopted by the school contribute to and support its most important goals.

To help you get started, Figure 2.2 shows an example of a completed worksheet. As shown in Figure 2.2, the *Academic* attribute directs the school's activities. This is demonstrated in the statement "Student learning needs should be the primary focus of all decisions affecting the school's work." An RTI process is consistent with this goal in that it provides a system through which student learning needs are addressed by a tiered system of instruction and intervention. RTI can also support the goal included in the *Personal* attribute, "Students need to be actively involved in self-evaluation and the production of quality work," if students are included in the process of progress monitoring. The important step here, though, is to ensure that the school has consensus on what the mission statement means and on how goals can be developed across the four attributes.

HOW IS RTI EXPECTED
TO LEAD TO THESE OUTCOMES?

In recent years, much has been written about the failure of many school reform efforts to fundamentally transform schools, improve student achievement, and reduce dropout rates. In trying to understand why so many reform efforts have not delivered lasting results, several policy researchers point to the disjointed incrementalism, fragmentation (Hill & Celio, 1998), and incoherence (Honig & Hatch, 2004) of these efforts. As individual programs are adopted, schools become hosts to multiple programs, each operating as if it were the only game in town (Hill & Celio, 1998). The lack of coordination of these programs leads to a competition for scarce resources and ultimately results in many programs leading to little progress (Hill & Celio, 1998). RTI as a systems framework has the potential to coordinate various programs so that they work in concert with

Figure 2.1   Organizational Mission Statement Planning Document

Our mission statement:

_____

_____

_____

How this mission statement addresses each of the four attributes:

Personal: _____

_____

Academic: _____

_____

Vocational: _____

_____

Social: _____

_____

From Johnson, E., & Mellard, D. F. (2006). *Getting started with SLD determination: After IDEA reauthorization.* Lawrence, KS: National Research Center on Learning Disabilities.

Figure 2.2   Organizational Mission Statement Document (Example)

Our mission statement: The mission of our school's faculty, staff, students, parents, and community is to provide a safe learning environment that enables all students to maximize achievement through a rich variety of educational experiences.

How this mission statement addresses each of the four attributes:

Personal: The commitment to continuous improvement is imperative if our schools are to enable students to become confident, self-directed, lifelong learners. Students need to be actively involved in self-evaluation and the production of quality work.

Academic: Student learning needs should be the primary focus of all decisions affecting the school's work. Students learn in different ways and should be provided a variety of instructional approaches, including the use of technology, to support their learning.

Vocational: Students need the skills (beyond academic) that allow them to be successful in the workplace and community.

Social: A student's education is enhanced by positive relationships, extracurricular activities, and a system of academic and emotional support. Students need to participate in extracurricular activities to develop leadership and teamwork skills outside the classroom.

From Johnson, E., & Mellard, D. F. (2006). *Getting started with SLD determination: After IDEA reauthorization.* Lawrence, KS: National Research Center on Learning Disabilities.

one another to achieve desired outcomes. For example, RTI can coordinate several reform theories such as professional development networks (or PLCs), standards-based models, early intervention, and DBDM. As discussed in the previous section, RTI can address many aspects of a school's overall mission and goals but only when these goals are clearly articulated and understood by all members of the school staff.

Because RTI is a systems framework, it can prevent what Honig and Hatch (2004) refer to as "policy incoherence." As a design for school functioning, RTI provides a structure that allows all parts of a school to work together to enhance student learning. As is shown in Chapter 1, Figure 1.3, initiatives such as PLC and DBDM are mechanisms through which the objectives of the RTI process are accomplished, leading to continuous school improvement. Throughout this text we discuss how the PLC framework can be integrated within an RTI system. Similarly, DBDM is witnessed in several components of RTI, such as the screening process—cut scores and associated decision rules (data) guide decision making about providing interventions to students. DBDM is also a part of progress monitoring and helps to answer the question: Is the student making growth when provided an intervention, or do we need to try something else?

The integration of RTI components with research-based initiatives is not limited to screening and progress monitoring. Each of the specific components of RTI integrates a variety of research-based initiatives that work together to lead to improved student achievement and continuous school improvement. School staff members need to understand how the RTI process works as a system and need to be aware of their own role in the system and in supporting student achievement. For example, general education teachers may not be aware that by integrating literacy across the content areas and by using differentiation and universal design instructional approaches in Tier 1 that they will support students who receive interventions for literacy needs (Tier 2) to continue to make progress in the general education curriculum. Similarly, grade-level teachers may view common assessments as an infringement on their professional freedom to instruct students, unless they understand that common assessments serve as an important way to align the curriculum and determine where supports for instruction are needed. Finally, intervention specialists may not understand why progress monitoring is important until they see that progress-monitoring data allow for immediate intervention adjustments *and* provide school-level feedback about the efficacy of a particular intervention.

In this book we offer explanations of how the various components of RTI can lead to improved student outcomes and have attempted to summarize our explanations in Figure 1.3 (see page 11). To answer the question at the beginning of this section—How is RTI expected to lead to these outcomes?—school leaders might consider engaging staff in an exercise in which they construct a shared vision and understanding of the process. Ideally, staff should also articulate how they envision their role within the process.

WHAT MUST HAPPEN
IF RTI IS TO WORK AS EXPECTED?

Once a school has defined its goals and has articulated an understanding of how the RTI process will support attainment of those goals, it will need to determine its own starting point for implementation. This can best be accomplished by conducting a needs assessment, a systematic study of an innovation that incorporates data and opinions from multiple sources to help leaders make effective decisions or recommendations about what should happen next (Wedman, 2007). A needs assessment is a data-driven process that can be conducted by or in collaboration with PLC teams. The data you collect, analyze, and interpret will move you through the process.

Data can come from interviews, surveys, observations, focus groups, product samples, and a wealth of other sources. A comprehensive needs assessment does the following:

1. Describes the current status of instruction, performance, and learning.

2. Provides an accounting of existing resources or programs available in the school.

3. Identifies "gaps" that allow school personnel to identify priorities for improvement efforts.

4. Presents results in a way that is useful for setting priorities, planning programs, and making other decisions.

5. Addresses component alignment and provides the "big picture" view—do things fit together in a way that will enable you to accomplish what you want to accomplish?

Steps in Conducting a Needs Assessment

In their text *RTI: A Practitioner's Guide to Implementing Response to Intervention,* Mellard and Johnson (2008) provided implementation checklists for each component in an RTI model. We have combined elements from their checklists to create a single checklist (see the Appendix) that is a good starting point for conducting a needs assessment. PLC teams can be designated for each component, and their initial task can be to complete the checklist together, collecting data to inform the process as necessary. Once the data have been collected, the building leader, along with the core RTI team, can review the completed checklist and determine priorities for getting started. An important consideration in this process is the acceptance that implementation and revision is a multiple-year commitment. For example, in a national RTI model site identification project, schools with successful models of RTI described implementation as a series of stages, building on the components that were already in place and targeting specific areas that impacted the most students first (Deshler & Mellard, 2006). For many secondary schools, this suggests that making improvements to the Tier 1 instructional program and developing universal screening procedures (see Chapters 4 and 5) will likely be good starting points.

WHAT DATA CAN BE USED TO INFORM IMPLEMENTATION EFFORTS?

Although conducting a needs assessment is a critical first step, implementation and continuous improvement require much more work than completing a checklist to determine compliance with a series of outlined steps. Careful attention must be paid to the sources of data that will form the basis of the implementation and improvement process. Data should be collected from many sources in an effort to provide a more complete picture and to avoid allowing any one indicator to drive decision making. Table 2.1 outlines potential sources of data for each component. As can be seen, data sources may overlap across components and are not restricted to test scores and other quantitative metrics that are easy to collect on students. Sources should also include qualitative measures such as observations, interviews, surveys, student input, and program descriptions. In the early stages of implementation, qualitative sources may provide more information since changes to test scores may not happen immediately. In addition, student input can be invaluable, especially as a school develops intervention processes and strategies. Students can be asked, "Does this intervention support your learning? If yes, how? If no, what else do you think would be helpful?" Student input is often an important source of information, yet one that is frequently overlooked during evaluating how well a process works (Fullan, 2001).

The important point on data collection is that by collecting a variety of data types from multiple sources and stakeholders, school leaders pay attention not only to the specifics of the RTI process, but also to understanding the values and context in which changes are taking place (Mellard & Johnson, 2008). Schools cannot measure the success of a new process based solely on its technical merits; they also must ensure that key stakeholders understand their roles and that the new process is implemented in a manner consistent with the culture of the school setting (Reid, 1987). As schools develop and refine their RTI processes, continued discussions of values and changes in roles and responsibilities may help facilitate the development of an RTI process consistent with the goals and mission of the school (Mellard & Johnson, 2008).

Table 2.1 Sources of Data to Evaluate an RTI Process

Component	Sources of Data
Screening	1. Results on screening measure 2. Tables comparing screening results with test outcomes 3. Student progress in interventions—are the decision rules appropriate? 4. Logistical requirements for screening—how much time, training, and funding are required?

Component	Sources of Data
Tier 1	1. National organizations and standards, such as the National Council of Teachers of Mathematics 2. State standards and assessment results 3. Teacher input on standards, curriculum, and instruction 4. Teacher observation 5. Literature and research on instructional practices 6. Student surveys—what instructional strategies are most effective? 7. Logistical requirements for Tier 1—how much training, resources, and funding are required?
Progress Monitoring	1. Technical assistance centers such as the National Center on Student Progress Monitoring—do school practices align with research? 2. Results on monitoring in all tiers of instruction—are students making adequate progress? 3. Logistical requirements for Progress Monitoring—how much time, training, and funding are required?
Tier 2	1. Student progress in the Tier 2 program 2. Performance on assessments—do students who receive Tier 2 interventions "close the gap" in their performance over time? 3. Research and literature on effective intervention strategies for struggling learners 4. Do the decision rules made during the screening phase seem accurate—are the "right" students being identified for Tier 2 intervention? 5. Student surveys—do the intervention strategies support their learning needs? 6. Logistical requirements for Tier 2—how much training, resources, and funding are required?
Tier 3	1. Student progress in Tier 3 2. Research and literature on effective instructional strategies for students with disabilities 3. Alignment of Tier 3 with the standards in Tier 1—do students have access to the general education curriculum as appropriate? 4. Student participation in transition planning—does the Tier 3 program support their transition goals? 5. Logistical requirements for Tier 3—how much time, training, and funding are required?

HOW DO WE DEVELOP A SYSTEM FOR ANALYZING AND EVALUATING DATA?

Many schools collect a lot of data. Unfortunately, data often are collected simply to satisfy reporting and other compliance requirements rather than to inform the process of continuous school improvement. Although the collection of data is a necessary first step in program evaluation, data collection that is not followed by data analysis leading to action is insufficient for conducting program evaluation. Just as a critical step in progress monitoring of student RTI includes the visual display, analysis, and evaluation of data, evaluating the process of RTI implementation requires the collection, visual display, analysis, and evaluation of data to make decisions. In Figure 2.3, the RTI Grades 6–12 Continuous Improvement Checklist, we illustrate a system schools can use to review and collect these data. The core RTI team, which should be involved in routine evaluations (at least twice each semester and as often as monthly), can use this system to capture a broad sense of the current status of RTI components.

The RTI Grades 6–12 Continuous Improvement Checklist (Figure 2.3) is broken down into four general categories: (a) general education instruction, (b) assessment, (c) interventions, and (d) special education. In the "Area" column, we have identified and listed the salient features within each category. Next, we've included columns for policies, resources, and training. The core RTI team can use a "red—yellow—green" system of shading in these columns to indicate whether the necessary policies, resources, and training are in place. For example, to complete the row for Item 2.1–Screening, if a school has a system in place to identify students who are at risk for reading problems, has the necessary resources to employ that system, and has clearly developed procedures for the process and decision making, the corresponding "Policies" and "Resources" columns should be shaded green. If the school recently had high staff turnover, the corresponding "Training" column would be yellow to indicate that new staff members required professional development for using the system. Data sources that would inform the completion of this category would be a review of policies and existing resources, past screening data, and resulting decision making (e.g., Do cut scores result in accurate identification of students who are truly at risk, or do they require adjustment?), and personnel records. Overall, the "Current Status" column for this item could be shaded green if the school has already scheduled the professional development for new teachers, or yellow if the school has not scheduled the professional development yet.

In addition to having a tool or checklist for the collection, visual display, analysis, and evaluation of data, a building leader will need to

(*Text continued on page 32*)

Figure 2.3 RTI Grades 6–12 Continuous Improvement Checklist

RTI Grades 6–12 Continuous Improvement Checklist					
Date: _____					
1. General Education Instruction—Tier 1					
Area	Policies	Resources	Training	Data Sources	Current Status
1.1	**English/Language Arts**				
a.	Research-based curriculum				
b.	Research-based instructional strategies				
c.	Accommodations for students receiving Tier 2 supports are provided				
d.	Common assessments used				
e.	Accountability measures show students meeting performance standards				
f.	Collaboration time provided				
g.	Horizontal alignment of the curriculum				
1.2	**Mathematics**				
a.	Research-based curriculum				

(Continued)

Figure 2.3 (Continued)

	Area	Policies	Resources	Training	Data Sources	Current Status
b.	Research-based instructional strategies					
c.	Accommodations for students receiving Tier 2 supports are provided					
d.	Common assessments used					
e.	Accountability measures show students meeting performance standards					
f.	Collaboration time provided					
g.	Horizontal alignment of the curriculum					
1.3	**Science**					
a.	Research-based curriculum					
b.	Research-based instructional strategies					
c.	Accommodations for students receiving Tier 2 supports are provided					
d.	Common assessments used					

	Area	Policies	Resources	Training	Data Sources	Current Status
e.	Accountability measures show students meeting performance standards					
f.	Collaboration time provided					
g.	Horizontal alignment of the curriculum					
1.4	**Social Studies**					
a.	Research-based curriculum					
b.	Research-based instructional strategies					
c.	Accommodations for students receiving Tier 2 supports are provided					
d.	Common assessments used					
e.	Accountability measures show students meeting performance standards					
f.	Collaboration time provided					
g.	Horizontal alignment of the curriculum					

(Continued)

Figure 2.3 (Continued)

2. Assessment

	Area	Policies	Resources	Training	Data Sources	Current Status
2.1	**Screening**					
a.	Systems (reliable, valid assessment procedures accompanied by decision rules and processes for collecting, analyzing, and evaluating data) to identify students at risk exist for the following:					
a.1	Reading/Language Arts					
a.2	Mathematics					
a.3	Attendance					
a.4	Course/Credit completion					
a.5	Behavior grades/Records					
2.2	**Progress Monitoring**					
a.	Curriculum-based Measurements (CBMs) are used in Tier 2					
b.	Individual students are making progress in the intervention					
c.	Progress Monitoring (PM) measures indicate general efficacy of interventions					

3. Interventions—Tier 2

	Area	Policies	Resources	Training	Data Sources	Current Status
3.1	**English/Language Arts**					
a.	Research-based interventions					
b.	Research-based intervention strategies					
c.	Accommodations in the general education for students receiving Tier 2 supports are provided					
d.	PM employed to determine intervention efficacy					
3.2	**Mathematics**					
a.	Research-based interventions					
b.	Research-based intervention strategies					
c.	Accommodations in the general education for students receiving Tier 2 supports are provided					
d.	PM employed to determine intervention efficacy					

(Continued)

Figure 2.3 (Continued)

	Area	Policies	Resources	Training	Data Sources	Current Status
3.3	**Engagement/Attendance**					
a.	Research-based interventions					
b.	Data system monitors intervention efficacy					
c.	Accommodations for students receiving Tier 2 supports are provided					
4. Special Education—Tier 3						
	Area	Policies	Resources	Training	Data Sources	Current Status
4.1	**Access to the General Curriculum**					
a.	Research-based interventions and strategies					
b.	Accommodations in the general education for students receiving Tier 3 supports are provided					
c.	PM employed to determine intervention efficacy					

	Area	Policies	Resources	Training	Data Sources	Current Status
4.2	**Alternative Curriculum**					
a.	Research-based programs					
b.	Aligned with general curriculum					
c.	Student outcomes					
4.3	**Transition Plans**					
a.	Research-based programs and strategies					
b.	Data system monitors transition planning efficacy					

Key

Policies: Does the school have developed policies that support this component?

Resources: Curriculum, time, software, materials.

Training: Involved staff have requisite training, and a continued system for professional development is in place (use green shading for in place, red shading for not in place, and yellow for in progress).

Data Sources: List the sources of data that allow you to evaluate this component. For example, the use of research-based strategies can be evaluated by teacher observation.

Current Status:

- o Red: None of the required elements is in place, and/or data indicate that the required element is currently ineffective.
- o Yellow: Most required elements are in place, and/or data indicate that continued emphasis is needed in this area.
- o Green: All elements are in place, and data indicate that the program as implemented is effective.

(Continued from page 24)

provide the infrastructure to support the process. Some of the logistical and administrative requirements will include the following:

1. Setting aside regular meeting times.

2. Ensuring team members have the necessary access to data and information that they will need to collect.

3. Automating as much of the process as possible to make it efficient and reliable.

4. Providing training to team members on program evaluation.

5. Ensuring team members have collaboration time to complete their assigned tasks.

WHAT SYSTEMS ARE NEEDED FOR CONTINUOUS IMPROVEMENT OF THE RTI PROCESS?

After each review, areas that have been highlighted as either red or yellow will require attention. The building leader, together with the core RTI team, will need to prioritize areas of focus, especially during the initial development phase. In other words, you will *not be able to work on all areas at one time*. Once priorities are set, a good system for action is to assign the relevant PLC team to begin working on potential solutions. For example, continuing with the screening example described in the previous section, a PLC team might determine that the most efficient way to provide professional development for new staff is to use the next in-service day to have experienced staff teach new staff how to use the screening process and materials. If a screening is scheduled to occur before the training, the PLC also might decide to have only trained staff administer and score the screen to ensure valid results.

It will be important for teams not to become complacent with "green" status ratings. Even if an item has been evaluated as "green," evaluations should still be completed to ensure it is still a "green." In addition, a building leader might consider rotating team responsibilities and/or team members for several reasons. First, over time, a team may become so familiar with a particular item and the data that it will be difficult to maintain the same level of intensity during the analysis phase. Second, rotating responsibilities helps develop broader understandings of the components of the RTI process across the entire staff. Finally, new team members may bring fresh insights on data collection, implementation, and refinement that can strengthen the RTI process.

Once the team members have completed the necessary actions to update the status, they can submit a brief report to the principal and core RTI team for review. At the next RTI improvement meeting, this item's status would be updated. This recursive process of action, data collection, analysis, and improvement is consistent with the PLC framework, shared-leadership models, *and* continuous school improvement.

SUMMARY

If the RTI process is not implemented correctly, it will likely not work. Beginning with the end in mind drives the setting of initial priorities through a needs assessment, and then sets the course for continued refinement and improvement of the RTI model. A shared approach to implementation and improvement that focuses on formative (inputs and processes) and summative (outcomes) measures engages school personnel in the process, which can lead to greater buy-in and, ultimately, greater success. Both quantitative and qualitative data should be collected from multiple sources and multiple stakeholders to inform the evaluation.

3

Leadership Perspectives on RTI

OVERVIEW

"Beginning with the end in mind" (Covey, 2004, p. 95) is advice applicable to school leaders starting the process of RTI implementation. As explained in the previous chapter, if a systemic approach to RTI is adopted at the beginning of the implementation process, RTI can become the organizing framework around which secondary schools align their mission, vision, and values with schoolwide programming. More specifically, RTI should become a *system* through which schools work to increase student achievement rather than operating as a piecemeal program operating in isolation. Although RTI implementation may seem like a daunting task for school leaders, it can become a comprehensive framework for meeting the needs of all students. In discussing the *Breaking Ranks* framework of school reform (National Association of Secondary School Principals [NASSP], 1996), Lachat (2001) describes the importance of this type of systemic reform, noting that altering one component of the school system affects other components as well. Therefore, piecemeal change can never be as effective as systemic reform.

The implementation of an RTI model can create a natural process for organizational analysis and evaluation of key school components related to academic achievement and positive behavior support of students. As a school leader, your challenge will be to manage, organize, and prioritize the implementation of systemic change.

School leaders are also charged with the important but difficult task of developing a school culture that is supportive of systemic reform. Change is often viewed as a purely technical challenge—do we have the resources and information to implement this new process? But an increasing amount of literature on school reform and change demonstrates that effective leaders also address the social and cultural values of an organization in order to guide the process of systemic reform (Elmore, 2007). Organizations that fail to consider the social context and personal values of its members *in addition to* addressing the technical aspects of change will likely not be successful in their efforts (Reid, 1987). Therefore, strategic models of RTI implementation address the required "investment in human capital" (Elmore, 2007, p. 2) by ensuring that the necessary conditions for implementation of RTI are in place (Fuchs & Deshler, 2007). As described by Fuchs and Deshler (2007), necessary conditions for RTI implementation include the following:

1. Sustained investments in professional development programs.

2. Engaged administrators who set expectations for adoption and proper implementation.

3. Willingness to stay the course.

4. Willingness to redefine roles and change the school's culture.

5. Providing staff sufficient time to understand the changes, to accommodate changes into their current practices, and to have their questions and concerns addressed.

Throughout this text, we discuss the leader requirements for successful implementation of the various components of RTI. However, building leaders may have questions about the overall process. In this chapter, we present and answer frequently asked questions about the role of the building principal in implementing RTI, drawing on information from building leaders who have been successful in this enterprise.

WHAT IS MY ROLE AS BUILDING LEADER TO IMPLEMENT RTI?

The role of the building leader during the initial launch and continuing development of an RTI model is multifaceted: supervisor, facilitator, and mentor. The building leader's role in RTI reflects the significant changes in responsibilities that secondary principals have faced over the last several decades (Portin, DeArmond, Gundlach, & Schneider, 2003). The most complex of these changes has been the increase in the number of issues for which the principal is responsible, which necessitates a movement toward shared leadership in schools (Portin et al., 2003). Shared leadership, which has been widely discussed as a way for principals to gain consensus among staff based on collaboration, is a means of sharing and transferring leadership responsibilities among administrators, staff, and community members (DuFour, DuFour, Eaker, & Many, 2006; Lashway, 2003; Portin et al., 2003). As discussed in Chapter 1, the PLC framework is an effective means of developing shared leadership.

The use of shared leadership models can be a great support for RTI. Although RTI can be implemented in many ways in a secondary school building, the process must fit the needs, goals, mission, and vision unique to each school. As school and district staff begin to evaluate, analyze, and examine the needs of individual students, the needs at the building level become apparent. Forming an RTI team that participates in all aspects of designing, establishing, and supporting the school's RTI model increases the likelihood of its success. The RTI team becomes its own PLC to work toward continuous school improvement (DuFour et al., 2006). The role of this PLC is the persistent analysis of the status quo and a constant search for better ways to achieve goals and accomplish the purpose of the organization (DuFour et al., 2006, p. 4).

Both the RTI and PLC models are systems-level initiatives that can work together to achieve common goals. For example, each model employs a problem-solving team in the continuous cycle of gathering data about students, developing strategies and ideas to support student learning, implementing these strategies, and analyzing the effect of the changes to determine what worked. Then, if additional changes are needed, the knowledge gained from this cycle is applied to make modifications, and the next cycle of improvement begins (DuFour et al., 2006).

An effective building leader under an RTI model will coordinate the efforts of PLCs (or shared leadership teams). The principal should keep staff focused on the school's goals of improved student outcomes. In addition, the principal will be primarily responsible for managing resources, setting priorities, and coordinating multiple processes such as researching interventions or specific programs for each intervention tier.

HOW DO I START THE PROCESS OF IMPLEMENTATION?

A building leader should focus on three main tasks as a school begins to develop an RTI model: (a) identifying the functions and compositions of the PLCs, (b) conducting a needs assessment, and (c) developing an action plan for year one of implementation. Each of these tasks is explained in more detail.

Identify PLCs

A building leader may want to identify a number of PLCs to begin the process of establishing an RTI model for the school. A problem-solving/data-evaluation team will serve as the core PLC for the process. Other PLCs may include one that develops common assessments in the general education program (see Chapter 7 on progress monitoring) and one that focuses on instructional strategies such as differentiation and universal design (see Chapter 5 on Tier 1 interventions). With each PLC, it is important to clearly define the roles of each member and to remain consistent about their responsibilities. This is especially true for the "core team," which has the responsibility for analyzing and evaluating student data to determine appropriate interventions.

The core team should comprise staff who participate in every monthly meeting, who can evaluate the learning needs of students, and who are able to support teachers in the use of effective instructional strategies. PLC members may include district support staff, such as a school psychologist who has expertise in the area of learning disabilities and understanding student needs. The building leader's responsibility at PLC meetings is to create the infrastructure to hold them. This includes planning for resources, scheduling, and supporting staff participation. A teacher from each grade level should participate, though this might be a rotating position; in other words, the same teacher would not have to serve for the entire year but could share the responsibility with grade-level colleagues. Allowing such a rotation can ensure that all staff have the opportunity to participate on the core team to understand how the process works.

Conduct a Needs Assessment

As a school leader, there is no denying that the word "change" can be interpreted by staff as negative and the initial reaction can be one of resistance. The most important tool to prepare an organization for change and alleviate some of that resistance is to assess conditions for change for launching a new initiative (Lachat, 2001). An assessment of current schoolwide practices provides data that a building leader can use to prioritize next steps. A needs assessment also serves as the initial step for involving the entire staff in the process of change. Mellard and Johnson (2008) have developed RTI implementation checklists that include measures for determining the current stage of development of specific RTI components in a school. Our version of their checklists is included in the Appendix. The first task of the PLCs should be to conduct the needs assessment using this checklist.

In addition, all staff and parents should participate in the needs assessment through a comprehensive school survey. This survey should include questions related to academics, school climate, behavior, resources, community relations, and out-of-school programs. Once data from this survey have been compiled, the building leader uses both assessments to identify areas of strength on which the school can build and areas for improvement. A sample survey for parents is included in Figure 3.1.

Figure 3.1   Cheyenne Mountain Junior High Parent Survey

Cheyenne Mountain Junior High Parent Survey

The Building Accreditation Accountability and Advisory Committee (BAAAC) Survey is your chance to let our school receive your feedback on its ability to meet your child's/children's needs. The BAAAC Committee is comprised of parents, school staff, and community members that discuss, review, and evaluate all aspects of our school, including programs, curriculum, and student achievement. Future goals and improvement plans for the junior high will be based on the results of this survey. Your opinion counts! Thank you for taking the time to complete this survey.

Please use the attached Scantron sheet to answer questions 1–51.

1. Student's Grade Level (mark "A" for seventh grade or "B" for eighth grade)
2. Student's Sex (mark "A" for male or "B" for female)

PTO/Other Committees

(Mark "A" for yes or "B" for no.)

3. I read the school newsletter.
4. I would be satisfied with an electronic school newsletter.
5. I would like to serve on the Building Accountability Committee.
6. I am aware of the district/school website and what information to obtain from it.

Curriculum

For questions 7–11, mark "A" for strong agreement with the statement, "B" for agreement with the statement, or "C" for disagreement with the statement. Please comment in the space provided for each "disagreement" answer.

7. Overall, my child is progressing academically as well as expected.
8. My child's individual academic needs, strengths, and weaknesses are recognized and addressed.
9. My child is being challenged academically.
10. My child's daily homework load is appropriate.
11. There is enough variety in the course offerings at the junior high.

Please rate your satisfaction with your student's curriculum in the following academic areas (A = excellent, B = good, C = satisfactory, D = needs improvement, E = not observed).

(Continued)

Figure 3.1 (Continued)

12. Mathematics

13. English

14. Social studies

15. Foreign language

16. Media Center/Library

17. PE

18. Performing Arts (band, choir, drama)

19. Visual Arts (ceramics, 2D/3D design, jewelry, drawing, sculpting)

20. Technology (applications across the curriculum)

21. Science

22. Special education

Comments

_____

_____

_____

_____

Home/School Communications

23. When contacting a CMJH staff member, I most often use the following method(s):
    A. Phone
    B. E-mail
    C. Written communication (note, letter)
    D. Conference

For questions 24–30, mark "A" for strong agreement with the statement, "B" for agreement with the statement, "C" for disagreement with the statement, or "D" if the statement does not apply. Please comment in the space provided for each "disagreement" answer.

24. I am satisfied with the three-week interval of schoolwide student progress reports.

25. I am satisfied with the personal communication I have received from staff about my student.

26. I am satisfied with the parent/teacher conferencing process.

27. I am satisfied with the access to my student's counselor.

28. I am satisfied with the process of obtaining make-up work from teachers.

29. I am satisfied with communication from my child's teachers concerning poor performance or declining grades.

30. I am satisfied with the response time from staff when I communicate with them through e-mail or by phone.

Comments

_____

_____

_____

_____

School Climate

For questions 31–44, mark "A" for strong agreement with the statement, "B" for agreement with the statement, "C" for disagreement with the statement, or "D" if the statement does not apply. Please comment in the space provided for each "disagreement" answer.

31. My child has had a positive academic transition from sixth to seventh grade.

32. My child has had a positive social transition from sixth to seventh grade.

33. My child's older sibling has had a positive academic transition from the junior high to the high school.

34. My child's older sibling has had a positive social transition from the junior high to the high school.

35. I am satisfied with the information provided to prepare my child for the high school.

36. I am satisfied with the disciplinary actions/policies implemented at the junior high.

37. I feel that harassment is addressed appropriately at CMJH.

38. I am aware of the tools that my child has been taught at CMJH to address harassment/bullying.

39. My child enjoys attending school at CMJH.

40. My child feels safe at CMJH.

41. I am satisfied with the school lunch program.

42. My child takes advantage of the before- and after-school time when teachers are available.

43. My child takes advantage of the counselors when social or academic issues arise.

44. My child feels comfortable talking with administration when social or academic issues arise.

(Continued)

Figure 3.1 (Continued)

Comments

_____

_____

_____

_____

Staff

For questions 45–51, mark "A" for strong agreement with the statement, "B" for agreement with the statement, "C" for disagreement with the statement, or "D" if the statement doesn't apply. Please comment in the space provided for each "disagreement" answer.

Staff members listen to my concerns and work cooperatively with me to meet my student's needs:

45. Administration

46. Counselors

47. Office staff

48. Teachers

49. Coaches

50. Maintenance/Custodians

51. Special education

Comments

_____

_____

_____

_____

Parent name(s) (optional): _____

Develop an Action Plan

At the conclusion of the needs assessment, the principal, assistant principal(s), and core PLC team develop an action plan. Including several staff in creating the plan is consistent with the model of shared leadership and also underscores the collaborative (rather than top-down) nature of the RTI process. A schoolwide action plan should include the following components:

1. A description of the expected benefits, objectives, and purpose of the shift to RTI.

2. A list of indicators that were used to guide the action plan.

3. A projection of expected short-term, incremental gains.

4. A realistic timeline for implementation.

5. A list of roles and responsibilities for staff as they relate to RTI.

6. A plan for regular monitoring to inform the process.

7. A plan for a coordinated professional development process to support implementation.

8. A process for maintaining continuing communication to ensure that staff are involved, understand the process, and have an opportunity to voice concerns. (Lachat, 2001)

WHAT WILL THE PROFESSIONAL DEVELOPMENT NEEDS BE?

Professional Development for the Principal

Principals will require professional development in the PLC framework as well as in the specifics of RTI. In addition, as the implementation process progresses, principals will notice the increased importance of evaluation, both formal and informal. This includes the use of formative and summative assessments for use in all areas of school functioning. At Tier 1, principals will need to learn effective methods to evaluate teacher performance in ways that support RTI implementation and promote collaborative processes. Related to this, principals will need to develop strong knowledge of and facility with instructional strategies such as differentiation so that they can support teachers instructionally. Tier 2 and Tier 3 require knowledge of progress monitoring and the management of that system at the school level.

Professional Development for Staff

As the core team begins the process of discussing RTI implementation, professional development needs should quickly align with areas projected on the needs assessment. For example, if the needs assessment identifies that the school lacks interventions to support student reading, math, or writing, teachers responsible for implementing such interventions will require professional development in these areas. If schools do not already use a process of progress monitoring, professional development will be needed in this area. It will be important to ensure that the professional development is aligned with the systems and interventions the school is using. For example, in a district that uses AIMSweb for progress monitoring, training on that particular system will be important.

It is impossible to recommend a standard sequence of professional development topics here because each building's needs will vary. The important point is that the needs assessment and action plan will help each school determine its unique professional development needs. Principals also might consider requiring that teacher requests to attend professional development opportunities be accompanied by a rationale of how the opportunity supports the school's RTI framework. Alternatively, principals might require staff to develop a longer range, coordinated, professional development plan that supports RTI implementation.

RTI FOCUSES ON ACADEMICS: WHAT ABOUT BEHAVIOR?

As described in Chapter 1, in this book we conceptualize a model of RTI that focuses on academics and behavior. Many secondary schools have a strong focus on academics because of high-stakes accountability and in the past have focused on a punitive approach to behavior. One of the many potential benefits of RTI is that it moves schools away from a "wait-to-fail" model and allows for proactive instruction, early intervention, and prevention. However, the wait-to-fail model applies to more than just academics. Through the use of a PBIS model as a part of the RTI process, schools can develop a *universal* and proactive approach to improve both behavior and academics.

The core RTI team should use the expertise of its team members who regularly practice aspects of behavioral modification to investigate current behavioral models created for schools, such as the PBIS model. These suggestions and models will most likely create an uncomfortable paradigm shift for some staff members. Moving from a reactive to a more proactive approach to discipline requires practices such as clearly defined student expectations that focus on catching students doing something right (the positive, in PBIS). This requires a schoolwide development and adoption of common standards and expectations for student behavior.

The National Technical Assistance Center on PBIS provides comprehensive resources for schools interested in implementing a schoolwide model of positive behavior (see the Resources section of this text). As a starting point, the PBIS center identifies seven main components of an effective PBIS model: (a) a common approach to discipline, (b) a positive statement of purpose, (c) a small number of positively stated expectations for all students, (d) procedures for teaching these expectations, (e) a continuum of procedures for encouraging maintenance of outcomes, (f) a continuum of procedures for discouraging displays of rule-violating behavior, and (g) procedures for monitoring and evaluating the effectiveness of the discipline system on a regular and frequent basis (http://www.pbis.org). In addition, this website offers many resources on PBIS functions within the RTI framework.

WHAT IF WE IDENTIFY TOO
MANY KIDS IN NEED OF INTERVENTION?

If too many students are identified as in need of intervention, this suggests that the core program may need adjustment. Recommendations for RTI implementation state that eighty to eighty-five percent of students should make adequate progress with a strong core (Tier 1) program. About fifteen to twenty percent of students will require more intense interventions provided at either Tier 2 or 3. If significantly more than twenty percent of students are identified as in need of intervention, a school's first priority should be improving the Tier 1 program.

Even with a strong core program, managing Tier 2 will likely be one of the most difficult aspects of RTI at the secondary level and will be a continuous struggle even after the system has been in place several years. Several strategies for managing the potentially large number of students in need of intervention are available. The first two are directly related to the effective management of Tier 2. The use of objective screening processes (described in Chapter 4) is a critical first step. Objective data accompanied by clear decision rules should be used to identify students in need of intervention. These decisions cannot be based on teacher referral (without supporting evidence). The results of screening then guide intervention development. Screening helps to identify not only an individual student's needs, but also helps a school plan for school-level resources. For example, reading support is likely an area of concern that will be shared by most students who are identified as in need of academic support. If screening data confirm this, schools should invest in effective, standardized protocols that address reading. More information on interventions is provided in Chapter 6.

A third effective strategy consists of assigning staff to serve as mentors for students who receive Tier 2 or Tier 3 interventions. Because the counseling staff can become overwhelmed with the time requirements of each student's interventions, assigning a teacher mentor who has a strong connection with the student increases the likelihood that the intervention will be successful by ensuring that students do not fall through the cracks. It also helps teachers become familiar with tiered interventions and progress monitoring. Some teachers may require training to fulfill the role of teacher-mentor, but connecting teachers with students in need of support is worth the investment. Teacher-mentors who track specific students also can prevent system "clogs" caused by a bottleneck of students requiring intervention or a breakdown in the progress monitoring system. These minor setbacks will occur, but if they occur too early and too often in the beginning phase of RTI, the result will be the slow death of support for RTI among staff and parents. Sustaining an effective and efficient RTI process within a middle or high school is the most critical role the principal has.

WHAT RESOURCES WILL I NEED TO PROVIDE?

Resources can be organized into three main areas: (a) professional development, (b) materials and equipment, and (c) infrastructure. Professional development is discussed above. Specific resources, including materials and equipment, for each component are discussed in the relevant chapters of this text.

Creating the infrastructure to support RTI will depend largely on issues such as scheduling, assigning roles and responsibilities, and coordinating meetings and other aspects of school functioning under the RTI framework. For example, to ensure that the PLC framework is effective, staff will need regular, dedicated time periods to collaborate and communicate. Some suggestions for allocating time include providing teachers within a grade level (e.g., all ninth-grade teachers) to have some shared time to discuss the students they have in common. This allows them to review data regarding student performance across content areas and interventions (if applicable). In addition, collaborative planning time for teachers within a department (e.g., mathematics) can create opportunities for teachers to collaborate on issues related to instruction and assessment. Although such scheduling is not easy to arrange, without some collaborative time, the process will not work.

WHAT IF I DON'T GET THINGS RIGHT THE FIRST TIME?

Remember that RTI is a dynamic, continuous process. Begin somewhere within the current system. There is no perfect formula for the perfect team meeting with a perfect plan for continuous school improvement. Although a wealth of technical information is available to support RTI implementation, when principals ignore the social context and values of the staff and stakeholder community, change cannot take place (Reid, 1987). In addition, asking staff to make too many changes at once can result in hitting a dysfunction threshold, the point at which people can no longer react to so many changes simultaneously and so avoid change altogether. RTI implementation will be an incremental and iterative process, and the use of DBDM and the PLC frameworks supports continuous review, evaluation, and adjustment.

RTI IMPLEMENTATION IN PRACTICE

Cheyenne Mountain Junior High School began the process of RTI Implementation in the 2004–05 school year. Figure 3.2 depicts a flow chart of how Cheyenne Mountain Junior High School began the process of RTI implementation.

Figure 3.2   Cheyenne Mountain Junior High's RTI Implementation Process

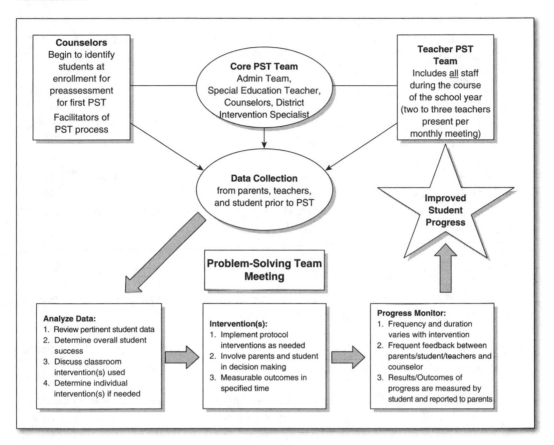

The principal of Cheyenne Mountain followed five main steps to begin the process of implementation. These are dynamic processes and decisions that need to be evaluated annually for effectiveness as related to the RTI process. In addition, other schools may find that a different process is more appropriate depending on the results of their needs assessment.

Step 1: Determine Core Problem-Solving Team

Remember that RTI implementation is more effective when administrative team members are a part of it. If it is important for the teachers to be a part of RTI, then it should also be important for administration. And, it is most effective if the same Core Team is used for each Problem-Solving Team (PST) meeting during the year. You will also need to determine any district specialists that could be a part of the Core Team and/or your special education teachers. A Core Team of five to seven members is optimal plus two to three classroom teachers. Include no more than ten members per meeting or the efficiency of meetings will decrease.

Once the Core Team is determined, include them in the following:

Task #1: Evaluate current practices used to assess student progress within the building, and determine how those current practices could be redesigned to fit within the structures of RTI.

Task #2: Determine how classroom teachers will be involved in the RTI process. The key is to involve them all to build knowledge and consensus about the process. However, in a secondary setting of large staffs, this may only be possible within a multiyear cycle.

Task #3: Determine the schedule (frequency and duration) for PST meetings (e.g., once-a-month meetings, biweekly). These decisions are important because they will be linked to progress-monitoring procedures and the review of intervention effectiveness.

Step 2: Data Collection Procedures

Using the Core Team, determine how data for each student referral into Tier 2 will be collected and managed.

Task #1: Determine individuals that will be responsible for taking initial student referrals and beginning the data collection process.

Task #2: Determine the specific forms that will be used for data collection. Look at what is already available online or from other schools. There is a wide variety of forms that have already been produced, use them! Much valuable time can be wasted on the creation of forms.

Task #3: Determine how and when parents will be involved in the RTI process. It is optimal to begin to include parents when gathering student data. Determine protocols for involving parents at PST meetings.

Step 3: Determine Data Analysis Procedures

Data analysis is the most important part of the process, but it is also the most time-consuming and most difficult to implement. However, it can be accomplished over time with adequate resources and professional development.

Task #1: Agree upon the data that should be collected for an initial referral. This could include information such as student history, summative assessments, formative assessments, and other tests that give an overall depiction of a student's academic performance and abilities.

Task #2: Determine how data will be distributed to the Core Team and classroom teachers involved in upcoming PST meeting. This can be a tricky task! It may take several different attempts to determine what works best for your team. Some possible questions to discuss with team members: Should a summary sheet be constructed and given to each team member before the meeting to aid in efficiency? Should the team collectively discuss the student's information during the PST meeting? How should parents be involved in this process?

Task #3: Determine who will be responsible for creating and presenting the data during PST meetings. This can be a labor-intensive process at the secondary level. Therefore, divide and conquer! One suggestion is to have counselors assigned to each grade level prepare their own grade-level referrals, as they know their own kids best. It is common in the high school setting to have more referrals in the ninth and tenth grades than in the eleventh and twelfth grades. Therefore, give consideration to workloads of the lower grade-level counselors and try to equalize the efforts of all counselors.

Step 4: Developing a Bank of Interventions

At the secondary level, it may not be common for schools to have a strong system of intervention and support. It will be important to determine the specific needs of your students in order to develop an effective bank of interventions.

Task #1: The most dynamic part of the RTI process is the development of interventions. Start small and remember that less is more in the beginning stages of implementation—there are no "silver bullets" where interventions are concerned. Begin evaluating what interventions are already being used in various capacities within the school. Evaluate, divide, and classify each one as either an academic or a behavioral intervention.

Task #2: Determine the greatest areas of need both academically and behaviorally in the building. Identify three to four needs each for behavior and academic interventions. As a team, prioritize needs for both types of interventions. Research possibilities that could be implemented within your building for the following year. Attempt the implementation of no more than two new interventions for each category.

Step 5: Determine Progress Monitoring Tools, Documentation, and Evaluation Procedures

Task #1: Based on the needs and priorities for intervention within the school, research progress-monitoring tools. The tool(s) chosen should frequently assess gains within major academic areas such as reading, writing, or mathematics, in conjunction with the interventions being implemented. This is an opportunity to receive input from district assessment personnel, other schools, or other educational assessment experts. The use of progress monitoring tools may take several years to implement correctly and effectively within the RTI process.

Task #2: Consider implementing readily available curriculum-based measures before investing in larger-scale progress-monitoring tools. This is a simple approach for the classroom teacher to grasp the importance of progress monitoring and its benefits for measuring growth quickly and efficiently.

Task #3: Align professional development with progress monitoring and interventions.

Process Summary

The steps and tasks described to begin RTI implementation within a secondary school will vary according to the unique needs of each building. It is important to remember that RTI is a systemic change that cannot be completed in a year. However, following these guidelines for starting the process will create important conversations about continuous school improvement. It is up to school administration teams and the Core Team to determine the systems and structures that best fit their school to sustain an RTI process.

SUMMARY

Successfully developing and establishing an RTI process requires strong, consistent leadership. The change will be complex, involving numerous moving parts to the system, a tremendous culture shift in the general education program, and an opportunity to integrate numerous practices to include not only what is helpful for students but also what is helpful for teachers. The building principal must understand the system, lead a needs assessment, and develop short-term and long-term goals and procedures to make implementation successful. The principal must keep staff focused on the school's goals of improved student achievement and will have to manage resources if specific populations require a higher intensity or different level of support than others. The principal will lead the integration of systems that allow the school to collect, analyze, and evaluate data at the individual student level, at the classroom level, at the grade level, and at the building level—and then prioritize and act on what should happen next. Most critically, the principal must create a climate of collaboration and shared responsibility.

In recent years, nearly all schoolwide reform initiatives have recognized strong principal support and schoolwide buy-in as key to the reform's success. RTI is no different—strong leadership is necessary if RTI implementation is to be successful.

4

Universal Screening

DEFINITION: WHAT IS UNIVERSAL SCREENING?

Universal screening is the assessment of all students to determine who is at risk for academic and behavioral difficulties. The primary purpose of screening in an RTI framework is to identify those students who, without further intervention, will be likely to develop academic problems at a later time. Screening measures are generally characterized by the administration of brief assessments that are strongly predictive of the condition we are attempting to identify and that typically result in classification in one of two groups: (a) those who are at risk for poor academic outcomes and (b) those not at risk for poor academic outcomes.

The usefulness of a screening instrument is judged by its ability to correctly categorize students into these two groups. However, no screen will be one hundred percent accurate in categorizing students; therefore, the goal is to maximize the number of accurately identified students and to minimize the number of misclassified cases (StatSoft, Inc., 2007). Accurately identified students can be either *true positives*—those correctly identified as at risk—or *true negatives*—those correctly identified as not at risk. Misclassified cases are either *false positives*—those students identified as at risk who later perform satisfactorily—or *false negatives*—those students not identified by the screen as at risk but who later perform poorly. Figure 4.1 depicts a hypothetical example of screening outcomes for eighty-five students; fifteen students are classified as true positives and fifty as true negatives. In addition, the screening measure failed to identify ten students

Figure 4.1   Two-by-Two Table of Screening Results

	Failed outcome	Successful outcome
Positive on screen	15 true positives (TP)	10 false positives (FP)
Negative on screen	10 false negatives (FN)	50 true negatives (TN)
Sensitivity = TP/(TP + FN)	15/(15 + 10) = 60%	
Specificity = TN/(TN + FP)	50/(50 + 10) = 83%	
Classification Accuracy = (TP + TN)/(TP + FP + FN + TN) = 76%		

who later perform poorly on the outcome measure (false negatives), and ten students were identified as at risk who did not need intervention to be successful on the outcome measure (false positive).

From these four categories, we can calculate a number of statistics that are used to provide an indication of how effective a screening measure is. First, the overall *classification accuracy* of a screening process is calculated as the number of correctly classified students (TP + TN) divided by the total number of students. In Figure 4.1, the overall classification accuracy is 65/85, or seventy-six percent. Next, a screening measure's *sensitivity* is the proportion of at-risk students who are correctly identified as such. In an RTI framework, sensitivity should be high, about ninety to one hundred percent, to provide intervention to students who require it (Compton, Fuchs, Fuchs, & Bryant, 2006; Johnson, Jenkins, Petscher & Catts, 2009). In Figure 4.1, the sensitivity is low, only sixty percent. We have failed to identify forty percent of the students who are at risk and in need of intervention. Finally, the *specificity* of an instrument is the proportion of students who are not at risk who are correctly identified as such. In Figure 4.1, specificity is eighty-three percent; we overidentified ten students as at risk who, in fact, were not.

In an RTI framework, the goal is to accurately identify students in need of intervention. Although, ideally, screening procedures would result in one hundred percent classification accuracy, there will always be some error. The goal is to identify all or nearly all of the students in need of intervention while minimizing the number of students who are overidentified.

WHY IS ACCURACY IMPORTANT?

The goal of any screening process is to obtain the most accurate prediction possible. However, there is little consensus on what acceptable levels of accuracy are. Although an eighty percent accuracy level sounds reasonable, what are the implications of incorrectly classifying twenty percent of the student population? To answer this question, it is important to consider the costs of screening errors.

Screening errors mean that a student has been misclassified. Misclassified cases include those students who are not identified but are in need of intervention (false negatives) as well as those who were identified but are not in need of the intervention (false positives). *False negatives* accrue a cost, because students who do not receive intervention early on may continue to develop learning problems that later become intractable. In reading, for example, this phenomenon is referred to as the "Matthew Effect" (Stanovich, 1986), where students who learn to read well early on continue to read and develop both stronger reading skills and background knowledge; and students who do not learn to read well at an early age avoid reading, read less, and fail to develop strong background knowledge and vocabularies. It is precisely this phenomenon that an RTI process can prevent through its focus on early identification and intervention, but only if all students in need of additional support can be identified through an accurate screening process.

False positives accrue a cost that is more difficult to discern in that they require the use of already limited resources for interventions that were not needed. Though most practitioners might argue that little harm is done to the student who receives an intervention that was not absolutely necessary, reviews of research on reading interventions for students in grades 5–12 indicate that the intensity and efficacy of interventions is related most directly to the size of instructional groups and amount of instructional time (Kamil et al., 2008). If a screening process overidentifies students as in need of intervention, the teacher-to-student ratio may greatly exceed those supported by research. This runs the risk of making the intervention ineffective for students who need it.

In summary, schools must adopt a screening process that allows them to identify all or nearly all of the students at risk while maintaining a minimum of overidentified students in order to effectively manage intervention resources.

PURPOSE OF SCREENING AT THE SECONDARY LEVEL

Although there are numerous important outcomes of interest at the secondary level, screening efforts should be directed to identify the following groups of students:

1. Students who are at risk for dropping out of school.

2. Students who have learning needs that require sustained intervention.

3. Students who are at risk for not meeting performance benchmarks on grade-level state assessments.

At the elementary level, screening is generally focused on academic checks of reading and math. The screening process targets these specific skills and directs students to appropriate interventions. At the secondary level, screening becomes more complex, more comprehensive, and requires much more of a systemic approach. Research on high school dropout rates indicate four patterns that emerge as early as sixth grade (and some research [Balfanz, Herzog, & Mac Iver, 2007] indicates as early as third grade) that predict higher risk of students dropping out of high school:

1. Academic performance track—Students who have a pattern of low grades, who have low test scores, who are failing core courses such as math and reading, who have been held back and who fall behind in course credits are all at increased risk of dropping out.

2. Engagement track—Students who have high rates of absenteeism, poor behavior records, and bad relationships with teachers and other students are at increased risk of dropping out.

3. Combined track—Sometimes the academic or engagement track emerges as a distinct problem, but at other points and for some students the tracks may merge: Students will have poor academic performance and poor engagement records.

4. Transition years track—Students who experience sharp declines in performance as they transition from elementary to middle school and from middle to high school are highly likely to drop out of school. For example, research on transition from middle to high school indicates that low attendance during the first 30 days of ninth grade is a more powerful predictor than any eighth-grade factor, including test scores, age, and academic failure (Jerald, 2006). Similarly, for sixth graders, any one of the following four factors significantly affects graduation rates: (a) low attendance (eighty percent or below), (b) failing math, (c) failing English, and (d) failing behavior marks. (Balfanz, Herzog, & Mac Iver, 2007)

Screening, therefore, needs to include the specific indicators that are the best predictors of determining students at risk for eventually dropping out of school. Achieving this goal requires conceptualizing RTI as systems change as opposed to piecemeal reform. For example, using poor assessment performance in prior grades as a predictor of poor performance in later grades may be a cheap and fast way to attempt to identify students who are at risk, but research shows that the reality is much more complicated. In some studies, grades earned in sixth grade were more predictive of graduation rates than performance on test scores in sixth grade (Jerald, 2007).

Screening instruments are devised to be brief and efficient assessments that accurately identify students who may be at risk for failure. At the middle and high school levels, the screening process will likely comprise multiple measures that inform decision making for individual students and for the school. Examining risk factors at the individual student level can help in determining the type of individual intervention a particular student might need. Looking at the aggregate of these factors can assist school planning efforts to determine when group interventions might be required. For example, a school that has a high number of students who are reading well below grade-level performance standards would need to invest in interventions that support struggling adolescent readers. Likewise, a school that encounters a high number of students with behavior or motivation issues might consider group interventions that target these skills. Similarly, examining data collected at the transition years (sixth grade and ninth grade) not only helps identify the individual student in need of support but also can guide school improvement efforts. A school that has a high number of students who experience significant declines in performance during their first year at that school will want to research and invest in interventions that have been demonstrated to improve student achievement in transition years. Chapter 6 includes more information about research-based interventions.

WHAT DATA SHOULD BE COLLECTED?

Because of the many decisions that will be made based on data collected during screening, screening at secondary levels must be both a systems-level process and a means of targeting individual students in need of support. At a systems level, maintaining data on research-identified factors most predictive of dropping out of school is critical. These factors include the following:

1. Accurate enrollment information, which is obtained through the use of a unique student identification number. This includes when the student entered the district, the number of times they have moved, and when they left the district.

2. Transcript information, which includes courses attempted, courses completed, grades in core courses such as English and math, credits earned (high school), and whether and how many times the student has been retained.

3. Attendance information, which is broken down by semester (or trimester) and includes a way to flag students who miss a specified number of days that puts them at risk for losing course credit.

4. Behavior grades or discipline records that indicate whether the student has significant discipline infractions and allow review for a pattern of behavioral concerns. (Jerald, 2006)

The development of this type of database provides schools the opportunities to then review individual performance data and to analyze trends and patterns that can lead to decisions regarding school improvement. Over time, the construction of this type of database provides longitudinal data—as students progress through the system, their status as a "graduate," a "transfer," or a "dropout" should be recorded to allow schools to analyze the predictive power of the factors at their school. In addition, if accompanied by data on interventions, the database can be used to track the efficacy of a school's intervention efforts. The National High School Center has developed a database called the Early Warning System (EWS) Tool that can be downloaded from their website (see the Resources section of this text). The EWS is formatted to flag students who have one or more of the risk indicators listed above.

At the more immediate level, screening tools that target the specific academic and behavioral skills can direct decision making on interventions for individual students and for school planning. Results on these measures should also be included in the database—this provides schools the ability to analyze decision rules and cut scores. The remainder of this chapter discusses specific screening instruments; refer to Chapter 2 for an in-depth discussion of a systems-level database.

IMPLEMENTATION

Before a screening instrument can be developed or used, it is important to ask and answer the following questions:

1. What is the outcome we are trying to predict?

2. How is unsatisfactory performance on this outcome defined?

3. What instruments or tools and related cut scores and decision rules will we use?

4. What are our next steps after the screening is completed?

Each of these questions is addressed below.

What is the Outcome We Are Trying to Predict?

As noted in an earlier section of this chapter, the outcomes we are trying to predict at the secondary level include both long-term (e.g., high school completion) and short-term outcomes (e.g., successful performance on a math assessment). Figure 4.2 shows a timeline of events that represent significant outcomes for both middle and high school students. The timeline demonstrates how outcomes are related to one another and how predicting and intervening to promote positive short-term outcomes can

Figure 4.2   Short- and Long-Term Outcomes

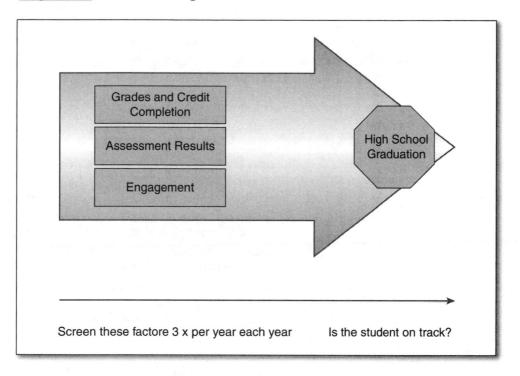

Grades and Credit Completion

Assessment Results

Engagement

High School Graduation

Screen these factore 3 x per year each year   Is the student on track?

support the long-term outcome, keeping more students in school for successful completion.

Given that the purpose of screens is to predict an outcome months or years in advance (Jenkins & Johnson, 2008), the first step in creating a screen is to define the future outcome the screen seeks to predict (e.g., high school completion). At secondary levels, we will be interested in predicting long-term outcomes, such as high school completion, as well as short-term outcomes, such as performance on end-of-year state assessments and engagement in school, that serve as risk factors in predicting whether students are in danger of dropping out of high school (see Figure 4.2). In most secondary schools, reading, writing, and math performance will be the academic outcomes of highest interest for instruction and intervention given their importance across the curriculum, as well as the research indicating that students who perform poorly in these key subjects are at highest risk of dropping out. Engagement factors such as attendance, discipline history, and performance in elective classes also will be a high priority given their strong relationship to successful high school completion (Jerald, 2006).

How Is Unsatisfactory Performance on This Outcome Defined?

The way in which outcomes are defined will affect the screening measures used. Earlier in this chapter, we described three categories of students that a screening procedure should provide information about: (a) students who are at risk for dropping out of school, (b) students who will likely require sustained intervention to be successful, and (c) students who are at risk for not meeting performance benchmarks on state assessments. Unsatisfactory performance for each of these outcomes will need to be defined before implementing a screening process.

Dropping out of school

In predicting high school completion outcomes, the first global outcome is successful completion of high school—does the student graduate? District and state policies will establish the requirements for successful completion. For example, most states have minimum credit requirements, such as two Carnegie units (credit hours) of math, for high school graduation (Education Commission of the States, 2006). Students who have failed courses in content areas that have higher Carnegie unit requirements than others are at increased risk for dropping out of school (Jerald, 2006). In addition, by 2012, twenty-six states will require students to take and pass exams to receive high school diplomas (Center on Education Policy, 2008). Finally, many states require completion of a senior project to include a research paper and oral presentation.

These requirements provide immediate and intermediate benchmarks that are linked to successful high school completion. For example, tracking the number of credits completed, especially those in English and math, will comprise part of the screening process and should align with the longer term goals. If a ninth-grade student fails to earn credit hours in English, that places that student at increased risk of dropping out. Intervening early with strategies that support the student's progress in English and successful attainment of credit hours can reduce that risk.

Students requiring intervention

This criterion is defined as students who will not be successful in the general education class if they do not receive intervention support services. Screening procedures targeted at the transition years of middle and high school help identify the number and type of intervention resources a school should plan for by considering such variables as (a) "proficient" performance on end-of-year assessments, (b) average or higher end-of-course grades, and (c) high percentage of completion of assignments and active participation (good attendance rates and few behavior disruptions) in the learning process. Students who will require sustained intervention also might be identified by reviewing information about their learning needs in Tier 2 programs at the previous grade level. For example, students exiting fifth grade who have been receiving intervention or accommodations in the general education classroom will likely require supports at the new grade level. Several studies have indicated that performance on assessments at the end of one grade level is highly (but not perfectly) predictive of perfor-mance the following year. Therefore, one source of screening information that will be helpful in identifying students who are at risk for not meeting performance benchmarks is their prior performance on state-level assess-ments. Other potential measures include curriculum-based measurement (CBM) benchmark tools in reading, writing, and math.

Predicting success on state assessments

This final category is important given the No Child Left Behind Act (NCLB, 2001) requirements that schools achieve high levels of proficiency and meet adequate yearly progress (AYP) targets. Performance on state and district assessments is typically categorized in levels such as "Below Basic," "Basic," "Proficient," and "Advanced." Students whose perfor-mance falls into the "Below Basic" and "Basic" categories have not met grade-level performance benchmarks. This allows for a categorization of students into two categories—"meets standard" and "does not meet stan-dard"—based on the assessment score (or cut point) that divides "basic" from "proficient." The goal with a screening process is to predict which students will fall into the "does not meet standard" category.

These definitions of (un)satisfactory performance now become the "criterion measure"—what we want our screening process to help us pre-dict so that we can intervene in a way that results in a positive outcome.

What Tools, Related Cut Scores, and Decision Rules Will We Use?

A screening process includes the use of tools such as assessments or the collection of data on specific factors and related cut scores and decision rules that direct what happens after the screening is complete. *Cut scores* are selected points on a test used to determine whether a particular test score is sufficient for some purpose (Zieky & Perie, 2006). For example, oral reading fluency (ORF) measures are often used as screening tools to determine whether a student is at risk for poor reading outcomes. A cut score on an ORF measure might be set at the rate obtained by students who later perform at the fortieth percentile or below on a reading test. *Decision rules* are agreed upon courses of action based on a particular per-formance on a screening measure or presentation of data. For example, suppose the ORF cut score from the previous example was determined to be sixty-eight words per minute. A decision rule for students who perform well below that rate might be to place them in an intervention that targets literacy development. A decision rule for students who perform near that rate might be to administer other reading assessments.

The selection of tools and the development of cut scores and decision rules are important and should be related to the outcomes we hope to predict and to the extent possible, based on research and evidence. We've discussed three categories of students we are most interested in identifying based on important school outcomes. For ease of discussion, we presented them as three distinct categories of students, but, in practice, there will be overlap. For example, students who fail to meet assessment performance benchmarks also may not receive passing grades in the relevant course. Tables 4.1 and 4.2 include a variety of resources to assist schools as they implement a screening system. The first table includes instruments by specific academic area; the second table includes information on constructing school databases that include academic and behavioral information.

Table 4.1 Screening Instruments for Academic Areas

Screening Instrument	For More Information
Category: Reading	
Reading Fluency & Maze Passages Florida Center passages Edcheckup	http://www.progressmonitoring.net http://www.fcrr.org http://www.riverpub.com
AIMSweb	http://www.aimsweb.com
Test of Silent Word Reading Fluency	http://pearsonassess.com
Northwest Evaluation Association (NWEA) Measures of Academic Progress	http://www.nwea.org/assessments
Category: Writing	
Direct Writing Assessment	See relevant state/district websites
CBM Written Expression—AIMSweb	http://www.aimsweb.com http://www.interventioncentral.org
WIAT II Writing and Spelling	http://pearsonassess.com
PAL (Process Assessment of the Learner)	http://pearsonassess.com
NWEA Measures of Academic Progress	http://www.nwea.org/assessments
Category: Mathematics	
AIMSweb Math	http://www.aimsweb.com
Michigan Mathematics Leadership Academy Math	http://mathassessments.mscenters.org/index.php
STAR Math	http://www.renlearn.com/sm
NWEA Measures of Academic Progress	http://www.nwea.org/assessments

Table 4.2   Screening Databases*

Instrument/Database	For More Information
Account from School Net	http://www.schoolnet.com
Data Miner	http://www.chancery.com
DataPoint	http://www.advanc-ed.org
EASE-e	http://www.tetradata.com
Early Warning System	http://www.betterhighschools.org
eScholar	http://www.escholar.com
Quality School Portfolio	http://www.cse.ucla.edu
Virtual Education	http://www.edmin.com
STARS	http://www.schoolcity.com
SWIS	http://www.swis.org/index.php?page=getSWIS

*This represents just a few available databases. For a more thorough review of these databases, see Wayman, Stringfield, and Yakimowski (2004) or http://www.csos.jhu.edu/systemics/datause.htm.

Collecting screening data on all factors for all students and maintaining the information in a comprehensive database can help create a system in which individual risk factors can be flagged for students. It also can help identify which students will require specific interventions and help leaders make decisions about how to direct resources schoolwide. Some of the numerous databases that are available for collecting and managing screening data are included in the Resources section. More information on databases can be found in a software review completed by Wayman, Stringfield, and Yakimowski (2004).

In some cases, cut scores and decision rules are not well researched and will require *post hoc* analyses of screening and outcome data configured in tables such as the one provided in Figure 4.1. For example, if a school has selected a screening measure to predict which students require intervention in math, but the screening instrument does not provide suggested cut scores, the school would administer the screen and collect results, and then compare results on a math outcome assessment later in the year. By comparing students who performed at or below a particular point on the screen who also failed the outcome, reasonable cut scores can be set. For other, more developed instruments, cut scores and decision rules are available and serve as useful guidelines that will require continued local scrutiny and evaluation (Jenkins & Johnson, 2008).

A perfect screen would distinguish every student who needs intervention from every student who doesn't—a black-and-white dichotomy with no shades of gray. Unfortunately, because the perfect screen doesn't exist, schools have to weigh the trade-offs of over- and underidentifying students as at risk. Two statistics, sensitivity and specificity, are used to gauge a screen's accuracy in classifying students. *Sensitivity* focuses on a screen's accuracy in identifying those individuals who later fail the outcome measure. Sensitivity is calculated by dividing the number of true positives by the total number of students who actually fail the later reading assessment (refer to Figure 4.1). *Specificity* gauges the screen's ability to identify individuals who will pass the criterion measure. Specificity is calculated by dividing the number of true negatives by the total number of individuals who perform successfully on the outcome measure (refer to Figure 4.1).

Sensitivity increases as the screen correctly identifies more and more of the students who have learning difficulties, whereas specificity increases as the screen correctly identifies more and more of the students not at risk. Sensitivity is easily manipulated by adjusting cut scores. For example, if we raised the cut score on a tenth-grade oral reading fluency measure from one hundred (twenty-fifth percentile) to one hundred thirty-one (fiftieth percentile), we would likely identify many more of the students who will eventually fail to meet the target at the end of tenth grade. The increased sensitivity would be offset by decreased specificity because raising the cut score means the screen will overidentify many students who are not really at risk for failing the reading assessment.

So where should we begin with cut scores? Most assessments provide normative data that can assist schools in setting cut points and making decision rules. For example, if screening in the fall with the reading passages on AIMSweb, schools might use performance at the twenty-fifth percentile as an initial cut score for identifying students at risk for poor outcomes on state assessments. In the fall of eighth grade, a score of one hundred thirteen or less on an oral reading fluency measure indicates the student is in the twenty-fifth percentile or lower (AIMSweb Reading CBM Norms). Over time, data collection and analysis might indicate a need for revised decision rules depending on how well performance on the screening instrument aligns with performance on the outcome measure. Maintaining a database and creating graphs and other data analysis tools can assist in this process.

To demonstrate this process, Figure 4.3 includes a graph of an eighth-grade reading screening instrument administered in fall and the outcomes on the state reading assessment administered in spring. As can be seen, the cut point that indicates the twenty-fifth percentile or below based on AIMSweb norms is used (ORF = 113). Successful performance on

Figure 4.3 Hypothetical Screening Chart

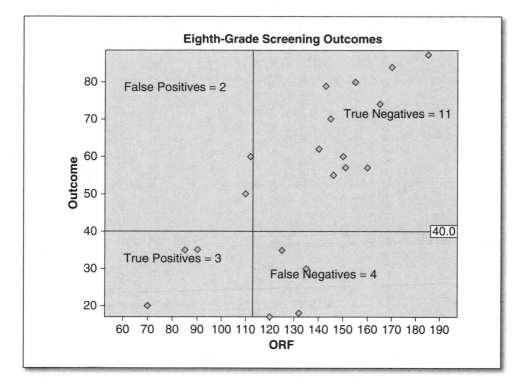

this outcome measure is a score at the fortieth percentile or higher. Using this combination of cut scores and outcome definitions, this screening process results in forty-three percent sensitivity, eighty-five percent specificity, and overall classification accuracy of seventy percent. Although the number of errors, six of twenty, looks small based on one classroom of data, if this process is repeated across many classes, schools, and districts, the number of errors can become significant. In addition, we have failed to identify four students in need of intervention, which suggests that adjustments to our cut scores are necessary.

Adjusting cut scores can shift classification rates. For example, if we raise the cut score on the screening measure in the example provided in Figure 4.3, we would see a shift in the number of students identified as at risk and, possibly, an increase in the number of false positives (e.g., overidentification). This is the iterative process in which schools will need to engage to carefully manage intervention resources.

Decisions about who, what, when, and how often to screen are complex. To illustrate the process more succinctly, we've developed a chart in Figure 4.4 that depicts this process. All students should be monitored with a system like the EWS tool. All students in a transition year (e.g., the first year of middle school, junior high, or high school) should be

Figure 4.4 Chart of the Screening Process

What Is Screened?	Who?	How Often?	What Tools?*	What Decisions Follow?
Dropout risk factors such as attendance, credit completion, course grades, behavior	• All students	Ongoing data is collected. Reviews should occur once monthly.	• EWS tool	**Systemic:** Review policies that support attendance; identify number of students requiring supports for credit completion. **Individual:** Placement in appropriate intervention (e.g., online courses for credit recovery; interventions designed to support motivation; meetings with parents regarding attendance).
Literacy	• All incoming students • Students who have been receiving interventions for reading • Students flagged by the EWS tool for credit completion or poor course grades	Three times yearly.	• NWEA MAP • AIMSweb • Florida Center for Reading Research probes • DIBELS • STAR Reading	**Systemic:** If numbers warrant, adopt a standardized protocol in reading (see Chapter 6). Review the core program to ensure accommodations are provided. **Individual:** Placement in reading intervention; ensure student receives targeted supports in content-area classes.
Mathematics	• All incoming students • Students who have been receiving interventions for math • Students flagged by the EWS tool for credit completion or poor course grades	Three times yearly.	• NWEA MAP • Project AAIMS • Yearly Progress Pro • Accelerated Math	**Systemic:** If numbers warrant, adopt a standardized protocol in math (see Chapter 6). **Individual:** Placement in math intervention; ensure student receives targeted supports in content-area classes such as science.

*The tools listed here are for illustrative purposes only; see Tables 4.1 and 4.2 in this chapter and the Resources for more information.

screened in reading, math, and writing. Ideally, all students will continue to be screened in the academic areas each year, three times per year (e.g., fall, winter, spring). In the chart, we have included examples of potential instruments to use for screening. There are numerous screening tools available; the examples chosen here are meant to be illustrative of the screening process and not conveyed as a requirement to use a specific assessment.

What Are Our Next Steps Following the Review of Screening Data?

Screening with one measure generally results in many classification errors. Therefore, schools may decide to adopt a more comprehensive approach to screening that includes triangulation of data or a multiple gate-keeping approach. For example, students identified on the initial screening instrument may then have their reading performance further investigated by looking at performance on prior year state assessments, district reading assessments, and grade point averages in English. If a school has a reading specialist at the secondary level, this person might also do a more in-depth assessment of students identified by the screening instrument to determine the nature and extent of their reading difficulty. Then, based on the individual student's need, a specific research-based intervention can be selected.

LEADER TASKS

An implementation checklist from Mellard and Johnson (2008) for universal screening is included in the Appendix. To begin implementation and coordinate the system of screening, in addition to using the checklist, a building leader will need to do the following:

1. Designate a "screening" team to review and select appropriate screening instruments (with district support).

2. Provide resources for screening instruments and database (with district support).

3. If possible, begin with existing data for the screening database to begin to provide longitudinal information on factors such as attendance and engagement.

4. Devote time and resources for data collection, evaluation, and review.

5. Ensure all staff are properly trained to administer, score, and interpret results.

6. Devote time to periodically review decision rules and cut scores.

UNIVERSAL SCREENING IN PRACTICE

The Moscow School District in Idaho is in the early stages (year 2) of RTI implementation. At the high school, the district identified a need to provide interventions for students who were struggling with reading and writing and decided to use the Language! curriculum as a literacy intervention. To identify students who need this support, a variety of information is used. Scores from the state reading assessment, the Test of Silent Word Reading Fluency (TOSWRF), and the Direct Reading Assessment, along with information about the student's attendance history, are collected. Students who have absentee rates greater than ten percent are not placed in Language! because of the nature of the program that requires active student attendance and participation. Students whose performance on all indicators is consistent with the cut scores are placed in Language!. For students whose performance is inconsistent across indicators, the school psychologist, together with teachers, reviews the data and makes a decision about placement. These students are closely monitored to determine whether they are benefitting from the placement. After the first year of implementation, the staff at Moscow High discovered that many of the students who were placed in Tier 2 intervention as a result of screening processes also had high absenteeism and were not benefitting from the Tier 2 program. Moscow High now monitors absenteeism, has changed its attendance policies, and includes interventions that address both motivation and academics for students.

At the junior high school, the district developed a similar process for math. In addition to prior state assessment data, performance on the Glencoe Diagnostic Test, grades in math, and a teacher rating of student organization and study skills are collected. Guidelines for placement in the Tier 1, Tier 2, or Accelerated Math/Algebra for students who excel at math are followed based on student performance across these indicators. Initially, placement was made solely based on state assessment scores, but the staff found that grades and teacher recommendations, along with state assessment data, resulted in more accurate decision making for students.

SUMMARY

Screening is a critical process in the RTI framework. At the secondary level, screening is conducted to determine which students require intervention and accommodations or support in the general classroom and to determine which students may be at increased risk for dropping out of school. Numerous screening instruments are available, but decision rules and cut scores will likely need to be local decisions given that different states use different assessments and have various requirements for graduation.

5

Tier 1 Instruction

DEFINITION: WHAT IS TIER 1 INSTRUCTION?

Tier 1 instruction is the instructional program that occurs in the general education classroom. Tier 1 is particularly important for a few reasons. First, RTI, with its roots in the preventive sciences, relies heavily on proactive approaches for ensuring high success rates in the general population. Second, the Tier 1 focus on *all* students is the most cost-effective means of addressing the needs of learners (Mellard & Johnson, 2008). Subsequent tiers address the needs of fewer learners with additional resources (Mellard & Johnson, 2008). For RTI to work at the secondary levels as expected, a general education program that consists of effective instruction and a system of schoolwide PBIS is needed. But what constitutes effective general education, and how do we know whether it is in place?

When Tier 1 is effective, the majority of students—about eighty to eighty-five percent—should be on track to meet state and local benchmark standards in the general education classroom (Goe, 2006). Schools that experience significantly lower percentages of students achieving benchmark standards may not have effective Tier 1 instruction in place. Effective instruction integrates the use of research-based practices across content areas to support the diverse learning needs of all students. In addition to the focus on effective instruction in academics, when RTI also integrates a schoolwide PBIS model, all students are exposed to a core social behavior curriculum to prevent problem behavior and to identify students who are not responsive to that instruction (Sugai, 2007). At the secondary level, the integration of academics and behavior can provide a strong prevention approach that helps schools build capacity to meet the needs of all students.

PURPOSE OF TIER 1 AT THE SECONDARY LEVEL

At the elementary school level, a significant focus of the instructional program is supporting the development of strong academic skills in reading, writing, and mathematics. The development of these foundational skills prepares students to meet the demands of the secondary-level curriculum. At the secondary levels, the focus shifts to developing strong content-area knowledge and critical thinking skills. Much of the work at the secondary level rests on the assumption that students come prepared with a strong foundation of academic skills with which they develop their understanding in the content areas. However, both veteran and beginning teachers find that helping all students meet high academic benchmarks is challenging under a business-as-usual approach to instruction (Nunley, 2006). "Business-as-usual" includes a heavy reliance on reading the textbook, answering comprehension questions, and taking unit and final exams to determine student learning. As evidenced by state and national assessments of student progress, business-as-usual approaches will not support the target of eighty to eighty-five percent of students meeting benchmarks in the general education program.

At the high school level, the instructional program is aligned with graduation requirements so that all students have the opportunity to successfully complete high school. Graduation requirements establish the goals for all students. In most states, students must successfully complete state assessments in reading, writing, mathematics, and science. Students must successfully complete a specified number of course credits in a variety of academic areas. In some districts, students also must complete a senior project to demonstrate their ability to think critically and apply knowledge to a real-world scenario. At the middle school level, the instructional program is designed to support students as they transition from instruction that focuses on foundational skills to instruction that further develops their content knowledge and critical thinking skills in preparation for the demands of high school. The purpose of Tier 1 instruction at the secondary level is to help the greatest number of students meet these goals.

IMPLEMENTATION

Big Ideas for Tier 1

It is beyond the scope of this text to present in-depth information on providing research-based strategies in the general education program. However, there are a number of "big ideas" in effective instruction that will serve as useful starting points. These big ideas include the following:

Literacy development across the content areas

Reading and writing skills are critical to student success across the curriculum and need to be an integral focus to "form a supportive web of related learning" (Langer, 2001, p. 877). Schools that have integrated the explicit instruction of reading and writing across the content areas support student achievement across the curriculum. Numerous publications are available to support a school's effort in literacy development (see the Resources). In general, research has supported the following main ideas for developing literacy:

- The explicit instruction of reading and writing strategies
- A focus on using reading and writing to support motivation and engagement
- A focus on developing student knowledge and understanding of essential content information (Torgesen et al., 2007)

In addition, when schools use consistent literacy frameworks across the content areas, students can more easily focus on comprehension and content knowledge—using reading and writing as vehicles to support their learning (Langer, 2001). For example, the use of graphic organizers to summarize and depict relationships across information (Swanson & Deshler, 2003), the use of "writing to learn" activities in the content areas (Graham & Perin, 2007), and the explicit teaching of comprehension strategies (Torgesen et al., 2007), are all effective ways to focus on the development of literacy across the curriculum. Allen (2004) has developed a concise how-to guide for teachers on tools for developing stronger content literacy.

Schoolwide Positive Behavior Support

Schoolwide Positive Behavior Support (SWPBS; Sugai & Horner, 2002) has been demonstrated to be effective at both the elementary and middle school levels in improving student understanding of expectations, reducing the number of discipline problems in a school, and increasing the amount of time available for instruction (Sugai, Flannery, & Bohanon-Edmonson, 2004). Emerging reports indicate that with some changes to the SWPBS model that address the organizational and structural differences of high schools, SWPBS can also be effective in moving toward a positive approach to behavior and engagement rather than a punitive one (Flannery, Sugai, Eber, & Bohanon-Edmondson, 2004).

Model practices of effective middle and high schools

It is always difficult to succinctly summarize what makes a school effective. Usually, it is a combination of factors driven by strong leadership and fostered within a collaborative culture of inquiry and support. Specifics are difficult to pin down because the system is seamless and integrated. Even though details will vary across school settings, a number of resources point to the following shared characteristics of effective schools:

- They set explicit goals that are aligned with state standards.
- Professional development activities are focused on the stated goals and support a culture of collaboration.
- Teachers take responsibility for the learning of *all* students.
- Students and teachers engage in active learning.
- Student data are used to inform decision making. (Dolejs, 2006; National Middle School Association, 2003)

Processes

The big ideas described above are used to guide Tier 1. The Tier 1 instructional program is driven by the schoolwide goals established within a secondary school and based on an evaluation of the school's historical and current performance across content areas and disaggregated subgroups (e.g., special education, English language learners [ELL]). For example, is there a pattern of strengths and weaknesses across content areas? Do the data demonstrate that students achieve at desired levels in English but not in science? If so, this can indicate that the school needs to further evaluate and adjust its science curriculum and instruction. In addition, does a particular subgroup of students perform at levels significantly different from the general population? For example, do students who are ELL achieve at rates that indicate that the school needs to incorporate strategies into their instruction that have been demonstrated to be effective for ELL students? As described in Chapter 3, it will be helpful for a school to designate PLC teams by grade or content areas to examine the Tier 1 program. If it is noted that a particular subgroup is not achieving adequately, a staff member with expertise in instructional strategies for that group of students should be included on the content area team (e.g., an English as a second language/bilingual educator should work with the team of science teachers). The process of ensuring an effective Tier 1 program begins with the teams' assessment of current practices, through which evidence is collected to answer the following questions:

1. *What are our greatest areas of instructional need across content areas and grade levels based on student data?* To answer this question, the team should review summative assessment data, such as performance on state assessments and final grades, as well as formative assessment data, such as performance on common assessments (see Chapter 7 for more information). Data can be evaluated by grade and classroom level to further identify specific needs. This review should also include an analysis of performance by disaggregated groups if applicable. For example, schools serving many students who are ELL should examine the performance of this subpopulation of students—is the Tier 1

instructional program supporting their attainment of established benchmarks at rates comparable with the general population?

2. *What evidence-based instructional strategies are effective for targeting these needs?* After answering question No. 1 (above), teams will then investigate various strategies that have a strong evidence base for targeting the needs identified. Sources of information include reviewing literature, networking with other staff and with other schools, and participating in professional development opportunities. For example, a team might identify a need to differentiate their instruction and focus on embedded literacy strategies across content areas because of an increase in students who are ELL, students who have not successfully developed the foundation of academic skills, students who receive special education services for mild disabilities, and students from low socioeconomic backgrounds. The team reviews and discusses these strategies and decides on a plan for strategy adoption and implementation.

3. *To what extent are the instructional strategies identified in question No. 2 in place?* This question is much more difficult to answer. Initially, a survey of teachers can provide some feedback, but unless teachers have specific knowledge of a research-based strategy, they may mistakenly consider what they already do to conform to research-based practices. This is especially the case with differentiated instruction and, to a lesser extent, with content literacy strategies. Additional sources of information to address this question include evaluating student performance data by content area and classroom as well as having an instructional leader with expertise in the specific instructional strategy conduct observations of teacher practices. By identifying schoolwide goals and gaps in the Tier 1 program, the principal can begin to help direct professional development efforts to support teachers who are making these changes. It will be important to conduct this step with a strong emphasis on collaboration and professional support to encourage honest and open dialogue among staff. Teachers should be encouraged to reflect on their current practices and engage in meaningful discussions on how to improve—this cannot happen if the principal does not create a collaborative environment.

4. *Do we have a clearly defined set of behavioral expectations schoolwide and a common protocol for handling discipline issues?* As noted previously in this chapter, improving the academic instruction at the secondary levels should be accompanied by a focus on establishing positive behavior supports. When RTI and schoolwide PBIS are integrated systems, the potential to realize stronger student outcomes greatly increases (Sugai, 2007). It is beyond the scope of this text to explain PBIS implementation. As with academics, however, the first step to establishing a schoolwide system of behavior is to gather information

about current practices and programs within the building. Such information includes current discipline records, a review of behavior and discipline policies, and a student and staff survey soliciting input on the development of school rules and common expectations for behavior. Once you have gathered that information, you can identify your greatest areas of need and prioritize them based on the shared values and culture of your school. More information on schoolwide PBIS is available from the National Technical Assistance Center on Positive Behavioral Interventions and Supports (see the Resources).

Once these questions have been addressed, the core RTI team can develop a small set of goals (three to five) for improving instruction. These goals become the yardstick against which all decisions regarding the instructional program are evaluated. For example, a school might identify the following continuous school improvement instructional goals (these goals were used to guide the process of Tier 1 development within an RTI system at Cheyenne Mountain Junior High):

1. Teachers will increase the use of literacy strategies across all content areas to improve comprehension, vocabulary knowledge, and fluency in nonfiction reading and to improve students' writing skills in the content areas.

2. Teachers will implement strategies that increase students' critical thinking skills such as their ability to summarize, analyze, synthesize, and evaluate content-area knowledge.

3. Teachers will implement differentiated instructional strategies to support the diverse learning needs of students.

4. As a school, we will develop and implement clear expectations for student behavior in order to improve student behavior, reduce time spent on discipline and behavior referrals, and increase student achievement.

Creating a set of schoolwide goals accomplishes many things that support effective Tier 1 instruction. First, the goals are developed collaboratively as staff members evaluate existing data on student performance, review current research on best practice, and consider their own current use of evidence-based strategies. Second, staff members' common commitment to instructional goals aligns the use of strategies across the school. This is significant, because students are better able to generalize and transfer strategies when strategies are used consistently across settings. Third, creating a set of schoolwide goals allows teachers to align professional development activities with the goals. Finally, this coordination of the general education program sets the foundation for the RTI process, increasing the likelihood of its successful implementation. In Figure 5.1, we demonstrate

Figure 5.1 Schoolwide Goals Development Process

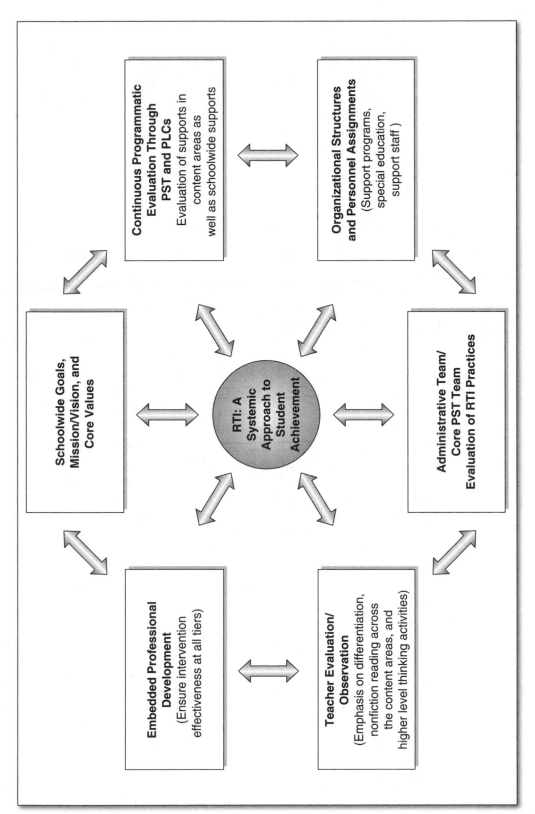

Continuous Programmatic Evaluation Through PST and PLCs
Evaluation of supports in content areas as well as schoolwide supports

Organizational Structures and Personnel Assignments
(Support programs, special education, support staff)

Schoolwide Goals, Mission/Vision, and Core Values

RTI: A Systemic Approach to Student Achievement

Administrative Team/ Core PST Team Evaluation of RTI Practices

Embedded Professional Development
(Ensure intervention effectiveness at all tiers)

Teacher Evaluation/ Observation
(Emphasis on differentiation, nonfiction reading across the content areas, and higher level thinking activities)

how the development of these goals helps to align school processes to support student achievement.

Once goals are established, implementation begins through the focus on (a) coordinating professional development opportunities to support staff, (b) committing to a multiple-year process of implementation and change, (c) supporting Tier 1 instruction through observation and evaluation, and (d) coordinating collaboration time for teachers to share lesson plans and discuss and review their efforts to date. The following section, "Tier 1 in Practice," describes the experiences of the staff of Cheyenne Mountain Junior High School.

TIER 1 IN PRACTICE: CHEYENNE MOUNTAIN JUNIOR HIGH SCHOOL

When Cheyenne Mountain Junior High School found that its status as a "high-performing school" was threatened because of drops in student performance on state assessments, the school began to investigate instructional strategies that would allow it to better support the needs of an increasingly diverse student population. The school first noted that in recent years, it had experienced an increase in the number of students who were at risk and noted that most staff members did not have adequate training to effectively support this population of learners. Through the use of the PLC model, teachers across content areas identified two main evidence-based strategies that were currently lacking in their practice that could support at-risk students: (a) differentiated instruction and (b) embedded literacy strategies in the content areas. The introduction to both strategies began with inviting local experts and district-level staff to conduct workshops defining the concept, establishing its relevance in the classroom, and discussing the positive effects of its implementation. After these initial workshops, a PLC on differentiation and a PLC for literacy strategies continued to research and identify specific strategies for all teachers and share findings at designated collaboration times.

Cheyenne's implementation of differentiated instruction began with simple formative assessment strategies such as the use of clickers to check for student understanding as new information was presented. Since that first step of implementation, the use of differentiated instructional strategies has grown exponentially to include the use of a variety of options for demonstrating student learning, integrating media to present content, and using a combination of reading and audio and visual presentations to reach all learning styles. More important than the individual strategies that Cheyenne has found effective, however, is the use of departmental collaborative time to discuss their findings, successes, and failures to work toward a common goal of improved student learning. For example, the implementation of these strategies quickly led to the realization that supporting literacy across the content areas was critical for ensuring high student achievement.

Through the initial work on differentiated instruction, the staff soon recognized the importance of continued instruction in reading and writing to support student learning in the content areas. For example, they discovered that whereas sixth-grade students at the elementary school were receiving approximately five to seven hours of direct instruction in reading a week, once they entered the junior high, they received no direct reading instruction. Yet, as seventh graders, students were expected to summarize, analyze, synthesize, and evaluate complex information across the content areas. This observation was supported by data analysis that showed that student growth in reading and writing stagnated once students entered junior high school. A PLC team devoted to improving literacy skills soon developed a plan in which all content-area teachers would begin to use strategies designed to strengthen prereading, during reading, and postreading skills. *Prereading skills* include strategies such as word/concept maps, KWL charts (Ogle, 1986), and previewing (Klingner, Vaughn, & Schumm, 1998). *During reading* skills include the use of think-alouds, advanced organizers (Swanson & Deshler, 2003), and question generation (Palinscar, 1984). *Postreading* strategies include retelling activities such as propositions recalled (Cash & Schumm, 2006), question and response (QAR) activities (Raphael, 1986), and the use of exit slips (Berglund & Johns, 2002).

Addressing writing in the content areas initially proved more challenging as staff reviewed a wide variety of writing formats that could be used in all classrooms. They initially rejected comprehensive writing models such as the Step-Up Model because they believed it would be too difficult and time consuming to implement reliably across content areas. To address the need for a shorter writing framework, the English staff developed a short-answer, constructed-response model that included a rubric for use across content areas. See Figure 5.2 for an example of this writing tool. Soon after its development, the use of writing across content areas increased, and, during the last two years of implementation, the school has seen a steady increase in standardized assessment scores in English and the content areas. Table 5.1 includes resources that may be of assistance as schools begin work on their Tier 1 program.

To develop the emphasis on improving Tier 1 and maintaining consistency across content areas, the principal connected teacher evaluations with the changes made to general education instruction under the RTI framework. For example, teacher evaluations now include a section that

Figure 5.2   Cheyenne Mountain Junior High School's Guide to the Short Essay

Cheyenne Mountain Junior High Guide to the Short Answer Essay

Every class at Cheyenne Mountain Junior High expects you at some point in time to write a short answer essay. You could be drawing conclusions from a science experiment, explaining the mathematical process on a story problem, or explaining the economic reasons behind the Civil War. *No matter what class you're in, the short answer essay that you write should always be similar in structure and style.*

What is the goal of a short answer essay?

Using tests, teachers can measure what students know about a variety of topics. Essentially, *short answer essays have two key components:*

1. Restate and answer the question.
2. Back up that answer with further explanation or examples.

How do you write a short answer essay?

Basically, you are writing a simple paragraph. You should have a topic sentence, main details linked with transitions, and—depending on the type of essay—a concluding sentence. Proper spelling and grammar matter. Ideally, your short answer paragraph should look like this:

Question   Why should Edgar Allan Poe be considered a great American writer?

topic sentence—restate question and answer it **detail 1**—reason, detail, fact, or quote **detail 2**—reason, detail, fact, or quote **detail 3**— (if needed) reason, detail, fact, or quote **concluding sentence** (if needed)	Edgar Allan Poe can be considered a great American author because of his range and his poetry. First, Poe wrote a wide variety of stories. In addition to writing in the horror genre, he wrote one of the first detective stories. Also, Poe was a successful poet. Poems like "Annabel Lee" feature traditional rhythms combined with dark themes. Because of these characteristics, Poe was one of America's best writers

Notice how the writer restated the question and answered it in the example. After restating the question, the author used the key word *because* which automatically set up the two main details that strengthened the response.

How do you write a topic sentence?

In the topic sentence, *restate the question and then answer it.*

Question	How do you think Thomas Jefferson's behavior as president might have affected the way future presidents viewed the office?
Topic sentence	Thomas Jefferson's modest behavior and belief in a small federal government may have impacted future president's views of the office.
Question	What happens to the energy from the sun when it reaches the Earth's surface?
Topic sentence	When the energy from the sun hits the Earth's surface, two things can happen: it can be absorbed or reflected.

What should you use for details?

- Try to use only two or three main details.
- Use specific examples, explanations, reasons, details, or direct quotes.
- Remember, even though your topic sentence may have answered the question, the details are the muscle of your essay. **It's not enough to have a one-sentence answer!!!**

Question	What happens to the energy from the sun that is absorbed by the Earth's surface?
Answer	When the energy from the sun hits the Earth's surface, two things can happen: it can be absorbed or reflected. When energy is absorbed by the Earth's surface, the land and water become heated. After being heated, the Earth's surface can also radiate some of this energy back into the atmosphere. Most of this radiation is trapped by various gases in the atmosphere. This type of heating of gases is called the greenhouse effect.

Notice the addition of details? Even though the first sentence both restated and answered the question, that wasn't enough. The details added both strength and insight into the response.

General Tips and Advice for Writing Short Answer Essays

1. A one-sentence answer doesn't cut it. You *must* back up your answer with further explanation: e.g., reasons, details, facts, or quotes.
2. Make sure your topic sentence restates the question.
3. Some questions have multiple parts. Answer every part of the question.
4. Be short and to the point.
5. Always write something. Never leave the answer blank.
6. Organize your answer by identifying all the major concepts and details.
7. Write neatly.

(Continued)

Figure 5.2   (Continued)

8. Spelling and grammar reflect on the quality of your response *in all classes*.

9. Always write complete sentences.

10. Reread your essay before you hand it in. Make sure it is *exactly* as you want it.

Sample Grading Rubric	Yes	No
1. Is there a topic sentence?	☐	☐
2. Does the topic sentence restate the question?	☐	☐
3. Does the answer include at least two examples of support?	☐	☐
4. Does the answer include correct spelling and grammar?	☐	☐
5. Does the response effectively answer the question?	☐	☐

Additional Examples From Other Classes

Math

Question: Allison is ordering copy machine paper for the office. She can purchase a 10-pack box with 200 sheets in a pack for $18.00, a 5-pack box with 500 sheets in a pack for $20.00, or a 10-pack box with 600 sheets in each pack for $57.00. Which is the best deal?

Answer: I decided that the best way to figure out the best deal was to find the cost per sheet in each box. I started by finding the number of sheets in each box. To do this, I multiplied the number of packs times the number of sheets per pack.

$$10 \times 200 = 2,000$$
$$5 \times 500 = 2,500$$
$$10 \times 600 = 6,000$$

Next I found the cost per sheet by dividing the cost by the number of sheets.

$$\$18 \div 2,000 = \$.009$$
$$\$20 \div 2,500 = \$.008$$
$$\$57 \div 6,000 = \$.0095$$

Since the second option is the lowest cost at $.008 per sheet, the 5-pack box with 500 sheets is the best deal.

From *Cheyenne Mountain Junior High School's Guide to the Short Essay*. (2005). Colorado Springs, CO: Cheyenne Mountain Junior High School. Author.

discusses the use of differentiated instruction (see Figure 5.3). Through the schoolwide focus on improving the Tier 1 instructional program, Cheyenne Mountain has been able to maintain its status as a high-performing school and has witnessed a steady increase in students' reading and writing performance.

Figure 5.3   Teacher Evaluation Form

Observation Feedback

Teacher: **Date:**

Evaluator: **Informal or Formal:**

Class/Subject:

Standard #1: Lesson includes components of effective instruction.

Student learning objectives were clear to students:

_____

_____

_____

Initial focus, appropriate delivery, guided/independent practice, monitoring, and closing:

_____

_____

_____

Lesson includes opportunities for students to demonstrate their learning:

_____

_____

_____

Standard #2: State standards serve as a framework for student learning.

Connects learning to district/state standards:

_____

_____

_____

Uses media/technology to enhance student learning:

_____

_____

_____

Uses a variety of assessments to monitor student progress:

_____

_____

_____

(Continued)

Figure 5.3   (Continued)

Standard #3: Advancing student achievement for all students.

Differentiated instructional methods are utilized in the lesson:

_____

_____

_____

Pace of lesson meets the learning needs of remedial and advanced students:

_____

_____

_____

Prescribed modifications for identified students were applied as needed:

_____

_____

_____

Standard #4: Creates and maintains an environment conducive to learning.

Classroom management strategies are effective, positive, and proactive:

_____

_____

_____

Students are engaged and are active participants in their learning:

_____

_____

_____

Teacher sets high expectations for student learning:

_____

_____

_____

Summary/General comments:

_____

_____

_____

Teacher signature   Date

Teacher signature   Date

Table 5.1   Tools for Getting Started With Tier 1

Strategy/Instructional Program Name	For More Information
Category: Research-Based Instruction	
Center on Instruction	http://www.centeroninstruction.org
Category: Differentiated Instruction	
Center for Applied Special Technology	http://www.cast.org/publications/ncac/ncac_diffinstruc.html
TeAch-nology Website	http://www.teach-nology.com/litined/dif_instruction
Differentiated Instruction	Tomlinson, C. A. (2001). *How to differentiate instruction in mixed-ability classrooms* (2nd ed.). Alexandria, VA: ASCD.
Category: Literacy in the Content Areas	
Content Area Writing	http://www.literacymatters.org/content/readandwrite/writing.htm
Content Area Reading	http://www.literacymatters.org/content/readandwrite/reading.htm
Content Enhancement Routines	http://www.ku-crl.org/sim/content.shtml
Category: Positive Behavior Support	
Schoolwide Positive Behavior Intervention and Support	http://www.pbis.org
Positive Behavior Supports Surveys (Getting Started With Implementation)	http://www.pbssurveys.org/pages/Home.aspx

LEADER TASKS

An implementation checklist for Tier 1 is included in the Appendix. In addition to managing the specific implementation tasks, the role of the principal is critical to the success of Tier 1 implementation, as he or she must provide both the long-term and short-term direction for curriculum and instruction for the school. To begin constructing an effective RTI model, the school leader must investigate and, if necessary, challenge the status quo within his or her building. Reeves (2002) compared the role of the building leader to that of an architect, whose most important contribution is the coordination of all contributors to a project (p. 13). This coordination helps create a structure that endures even after the building leader, or architect, has departed (Reeves, 2002). The Appendix includes a checklist for implementation of high-quality Tier 1 instruction, but the specific tasks required of the building leader include the following:

1. Provide the infrastructure for the initial needs assessment. This includes coordinating PLCs to collect and evaluate data to assess the current state of instructional practice.

2. Lead the task of establishing and prioritizing schoolwide instructional goals as a result of the needs assessment.

3. Connect instructional goals with professional development opportunities, especially during the early stages of implementation.

4. Encourage and support teachers as they begin to use new strategies.

5. Provide teachers the time to collaborate to further refine instructional strategies and create a systemic approach for achieving schoolwide goals.

6. Develop the infrastructure for continued monitoring and evaluation of the net effect of these strategies. This includes developing process for systematic data collection and evaluation.

SUMMARY

One primary purpose of RTI in a secondary setting is to help a school build capacity for serving the needs of an increasingly diverse student body. Because RTI operates under a prevention model of improving instruction and behavior, a strong Tier 1 (primary prevention) program that integrates schoolwide research-based practices is critical to ensure success. Building a strong Tier 1 program will be an incremental process that continues over several years. Schoolwide adoption through the use of the PLC framework and the establishment of a supportive, collaborative environment help ensure the process remains focused on achieving established school goals.

6

Tier 2 and Tier 3 Intervention

DEFINITION: WHAT IS TIER 2 AND TIER 3 INTERVENTION?

Tier 2 intervention is the instructional program that provides additional support to students who struggle in the general education, or Tier 1, setting. In Tier 2, students who are not successful in Tier 1 receive targeted intervention(s), and their progress in these interventions is monitored for effectiveness (Mellard & Johnson, 2008). For some students, Tier 2 interventions will not be sufficient to successfully meet their needs, and they will require intervention that is more intense in its intensity, focus, and/or duration.

Tier 2 at the secondary level includes research-based instruction, increased intensity of instruction with smaller groups, frequent progress monitoring, and an increased level of training of the professionals providing the instruction (Mellard & Johnson, 2008). At the secondary level, the emphasis of the instructional program shifts from learning foundational skills (e.g., learning to read) toward using foundational skills to learn in the content areas (e.g., reading to learn). Therefore, as students reach middle and high school levels, Tier 2 intervention should emphasize targeted literacy instruction (e.g., cognitive and learning strategies, comprehension skills) that can be generalized to and supported in content area classes (Shinn, 2005). In addition, because student engagement is a critical factor for high school success, Tier 2 intervention should also include strategies designed to increase student engagement and motivation.

Quality Tier 2 programming at the secondary level is important for two reasons. First, Tier 2 bridges the "instructional gap" that exists between Tiers 1 and 3. For example, with a quality Tier 2 program in place, students who do not respond to instructional practices in Tier 1 but fail to meet the criteria to receive special education services can get the targeted support they require. Traditionally, students who fail to "make it" in the general education setting are immediately referred to special education for an evaluation to receive services. This practice is unfair to students who are wrongly labeled in order to get the support they need to be successful in school. It also is unfair to students who do have a disability that requires the specially designed instruction offered through special education services. In addition, the practice of mislabeling students can be quite costly to a school district. Tier 2 intervention can replace this unfortunate practice, prevent students from being incorrectly labeled as in need of special education, and improve student outcomes.

Tier 2 supports students who struggle. Traditionally, students who require more intensive supports have to fail miserably for some time before receiving an evaluation for special education services (Kovaleski, 2003). This "wait-to-fail" model has serious consequences at the secondary level for students. Eventually, struggling students often fall through the cracks, become at risk of continued academic failure, and tend to drop out of school. A system of early intervention can prevent these consequences.

As described in this text, Tier 3 represents a highly specialized and intense level of intervention for individual students with disabilities. It may include placement in an inclusion class, one-on-one time with individual teachers, classroom observations, or behavioral assessments. In Tier 3, students may be working toward alternate performance benchmarks that are consistent with their Individualized Education Plans (IEPs). With quality Tier 1 and Tier 2 programming, the number of students who require Tier 3 services should be limited to students with disabilities.

PURPOSE OF TIERS 2 AND 3 AT THE SECONDARY LEVEL

Struggling adolescent learners require support to be successful in middle and high school. Without appropriate supports, struggling students are at an increased risk for dropping out of high school.

A main purpose of Tier 2 at the secondary level is to provide academic and behavioral support that targets skills and content that will support student performance in the general education class (Tier 1). Intervention programming at the secondary level includes academic and behavior supports that are research-based. An inherent challenge at the secondary level is the display of apathy and lack of motivation that teachers witness as students transition from elementary to secondary grades (Bridgeland,

DiIulio, & Morison, 2006). A lack of engagement can compound academic problems, and both aspects should be considered when designing a Tier 2 program. Tier 2 intervention must be designed to address the needs of and provide support to the fifteen to twenty percent of students who are failing to meet the demands and challenges of secondary school and consider dropping out as their only alternative.

Because the goal of Tier 2 is to support student learning so that they can access the general education curriculum, Tier 2 intervention will require an increased level of collaboration among school staff. The interventions provided in Tier 2 must target the areas of need and also must lead to increased access to and performance in the Tier 1 program. Therefore, in addition to training teachers on specific interventions to increase student literacy and use of strategies in the content areas, professional development must include coteaching and collaboration practices (Conley, 2008; Deshler et al., 2009). In other words, Tier 2 intervention at the secondary level will require a comprehensive approach that embraces addressing the needs of the whole student.

The main goal of Tier 3 in an RTI framework is to provide a level of services that is intense enough to support the academic and behavioral needs of students for whom Tiers 1 and 2 are insufficient. Tier 3 is reserved for a small percentage of students whose needs are significant and require specially designed instruction and/or a level of intensity that is so high that it cannot reasonably be provided through Tier 2 intervention alone.

IMPLEMENTATION

Tier 2 intervention is for students for whom Tier 1 is insufficient. Tier 2 is designed to support students who are falling behind on benchmark standards and require additional intervention to achieve grade-level expectations (Mellard & Johnson, 2008). Therefore, Tier 2 comprises processes and targeted strategies designed to enhance and supplement the curriculum and instructional program in Tier 1. What systemic, structural processes need to be in place to ensure successful implementation of interventions at this level?

Let's revisit the questions to be considered and answered by the team in Chapter 5 ("Tier 1 Instruction") to guide the decision-making process of potential programs or interventions for Tier 2 implementation.

1. *What are our greatest areas of intervention need across the content areas and grade levels based on student data?* To answer this question, summative data on student performance across the grade levels and content areas are generated. These data will include disaggregated academic performance in the content areas (e.g., grades, common assessments, observation) and behavioral aspects that affect student

performance in and out of the classroom (e.g., motivational issues, disruptive behavior, truancy). In addition, the determination of need should be guided by further inquiry into the basic skill levels of students who are significantly behind their peers (scoring below the twenty-fifth percentile) using data from standardized measures. Gathering and analyzing student data will guide the team in developing new programs and selecting the interventions needed to improve student performance.

Based on student data, the team will analyze and determine targeted problem areas for intervention and then design or select programs to support those areas of deficit. For example, let's consider reading comprehension as an example of an area of intervention for students who are struggling to meet the grade-level benchmarks in Tier 1. A targeted program will be developed or adopted that is evidence-based and designed to increase student comprehension of informational texts. The grouping of students should be homogeneous and limited to small groups, on average eight to twelve students per group. This small-group instruction is provided in addition to the core curriculum. The time allotted varies based on student need and structure of the program (this idea will be discussed in more detail later in this chapter) but will tend to be anywhere from thirty to sixty minutes in specialized, targeted instruction.

Student progress in the intervention is progress monitored. Recommendations for the frequency of monitoring vary but should be conducted at least biweekly to ensure adequate progress of learning and effectiveness of the strategy. If progress-monitoring data indicate that the student is not making sufficient growth, the student's intervention should be evaluated by the intervention specialist and adjustments made as necessary. The intervention period should equate to a typical school semester, be it a semester or trimester, but no longer without revisiting the student intervention plan and overall progress. The review of progress allows the RTI team to decide if the student is to be (a) exited from Tier 2, (b) given another round of Tier 2 instruction with modifications made to the plan, or (c) considered for referral to Tier 3. Interventions should be delivered by a trained professional (e.g., classroom teacher, reading specialist, teacher consultant, Title I specialist, and so on) who is proficient in the specific intervention(s) to be used. Any program or intervention adopted should be carried out using evidence-based models of instruction.

2. *What evidence-based interventions are effective for targeting student needs?* Tier 2 interventions are delivered in an explicit manner with more intensity to help students who need targeted strategies to be successful in content-area classes. The movement between the tiers should be fluid to best support, supplement, and enhance student

learning. Tier 2 is a temporary placement for students who struggle in Tier 1. Tier 2 differs in intensity from Tier 1 across the following dimensions: (a) focus, (b) grouping, (c) duration, (d) setting, (e) progress monitoring, and (f) delivery of the intervention. For Tier 2 to be effective in improving student learning outcomes, great consideration must be given to which instructional approaches will be implemented and how the specific targeted strategies will be delivered. The review and discussion of specific interventions is beyond the scope of this chapter. However, three main approaches should be considered to design and implement a Tier 2 process. These approaches are described below.

a. Problem-Solving Approach

Two approaches that have emerged as possible models of intervention within an RTI framework are the problem-solving and standard protocol approaches (Fuchs, Mock, Morgan, & Young, 2003). The problem-solving approach uses interventions that are designed to meet targeted needs and are individualized for each student. A team of professionals choose interventions designed to focus on a specific set of skills that need to be addressed. This approach uses an inquiry process that requires the team to evaluate student performance, identify the problem, and then develop and implement a plan using targeted interventions based on student individual needs and performance data (Kovaleski, 2003; Marston, Muyskens, Lau, & Canter, 2003). Because the problem-solving approach is quite flexible and can be adapted at any time to meet the individual needs of students, teachers find it conducive to the realities and demands of day-to-day instruction. However, the individualized nature of this approach also makes schoolwide implementation difficult—the logistics of coordinating several, individualized interventions can be overwhelming at the secondary level.

b. Standard Protocol Approach

On the other hand, the standard protocol approach relies on the use of specific interventions, typically selected by the school, to address the similar needs of small groups of students. This approach is much more prescribed and follows a detailed series of steps to evaluate, identify problem areas, and implement (McMaster, Fuchs, Fuchs, & Compton, 2003. Because this approach uses research-based strategies and instruction, it requires great consistency by those who implement the interventions. A major benefit of the standard protocol approach is the "streamlining" of Tier 2. One potential drawback of the standard protocol approach is its "one-size-fits-all" nature. For example, the *Rewards* program (Archer, Gleason, & Vachon, 2000) has a strong research base for improving the decoding skills of struggling readers. However, if this is the only intervention available for students, then it may not sufficiently address the needs of a student who is having difficulties with reading for reasons other than decoding.

Although the problem-solving and standard protocol approaches are sometimes presented as mutually exclusive, they can both fit within a problem-solving framework (Duffy, 2007). Many schools and districts use a combination of both approaches to best meet the needs of students. For example, as mentioned in the preceding paragraph, a school might adopt a standard protocol for addressing reading difficulties but use a problem-solving approach for students who also have motivational or study skill problems. The combination of approaches, especially in the early stages of RTI implementation, can provide a more comprehensive system of addressing student need until a school has the time to develop a "bank" of interventions to support student learning.

c. Strategy Instruction Approach

In addition to the problem-solving and standard protocol approaches, at the secondary level, a quality Tier 2 instructional program should include strategy instruction. Strategy instruction for struggling adolescent learners is research-based and has been proven to increase student performance. Strategy instruction is explicit, makes students aware of the purpose of strategies (how, when, where, and why to use them), allows for extensive practice of the strategy, ensures mastery, and actively involves students in the evaluation and modification of strategies (Pressley et al., 1992).

Strategy instruction models the use of cognitive processes that actively engage the reader with the text. The reader is involved in tasks that require them to activate prior knowledge, ask questions, make predictions, summarize what has been read, clarify information, and organize and integrate recently acquired information (Palinscar & Brown, 1984; Pressley, 2000; Snow, Porche, Tabors, & Harris, 2007). Researchers agree that the absence of explicit strategy instruction in the general education classroom prevents many students from performing at grade level and leads to gaps in their ability to read and write at the secondary level (Biancarosa & Snow, 2004; Deshler, Palinscar, Biancarosa, & Nair, 2007).

Teaching students to use targeted learning strategies in the core curriculum is possible. This type of student-focused learning includes explanation, modeling, and explicit application to content materials. Teachers create ample opportunities for students to practice using the strategies and provide feedback on their use as it is generalized to critical content information (Deshler et al., 2009).

However, as with any instructional process, targeted strategy instruction used in isolation and taught out of context without application to the content areas would be inadequate and miss the mark to properly support the targeted needs of students at the secondary level (Conley, 2008). Teachers must be mindful of how to teach strategies in conjunction with core curriculum knowledge and standards to increase student skills and performance.

These approaches—problem-solving, standard protocol, and strategy instruction—should be used in conjunction with one another to design an effective Tier 2 program that can effectively meet the needs of struggling learners. The Resources section provides helpful starting points for schools to become more familiar with each of these approaches and their use within an RTI framework.

3. *To what extent are these instructional strategies in place?* As described in Chapter 2, an evaluation of the current status of the general education instructional program, as well as the availability and access to interventions, is an important first step in the design and implementation of Tier 2.

In addition to assessing the existing instructional and intervention practices, RTI implementation teams should examine their current school infrastructure to determine how it supports Tier 2 implementation. The school infrastructure is an integral part of school functioning and contributes to the success of RTI implementation. At the secondary levels, scheduling, staff, and programming issues likely present the greatest challenge to coordinating Tier 2 implementation efforts. The changes to infrastructure that districts and schools can implement include the following: (a) extended time for literacy, (b) professional development, (c) ongoing summative assessment of students and programs, (d) teacher teams (PLCs), and (e) comprehensive and coordinated literacy programs (Biancarosa & Snow, 2004; Duffy, 2007). Factors that greatly enhance the likelihood of successful Tier 2 implementation include flexible or creative scheduling, lower teacher-student ratios, coordinated professional development opportunities, and integrated assessment tools.

One issue that will confront secondary schools as they implement RTI is time. To successfully complete high school, students are required to take a specified number of credits in core content areas. How can students who need additional support receive targeted strategy instruction within the framework of the increased curriculum demands and expectations and still earn a high school diploma in the allotted four-year time frame? The structure of Tier 2 intervention must include creative ways in which to deliver targeted interventions while allowing students to meet the requirements for successful school completion. For example, some schools have embraced block scheduling, allowing for more concentrated periods of time to focus on strategy instruction while helping students to apply core content knowledge. In addition, some districts have moved to trimesters rather than semesters to assist students in obtaining the required credits by providing more opportunities to earn them. Flexible scheduling is a necessity at Tier 2. See textbox 6.1 for a description of how Coopersville Middle School addressed scheduling challenges to design a Tier 2 program.

Textbox 6.1 Coopersville Middle School

Coopersville Middle School began the process of RTI implementation in January 2008. They were primarily interested in developing an intervention program to support the approximately fifteen percent of their students who were struggling with completing their schoolwork and were at risk for failing courses.

As is the case in many secondary schools, however, they found that scheduling issues were preventing the successful implementation of an intervention system. Their current approach to scheduling did not provide adequate time for teachers to work with small groups of students, nor did it provide the opportunity for grade-level teams to meet regularly to discuss and review the progress of these struggling students.

The principal, together with his RTI team, developed grade-level teams, each consisting of seven or eight teachers, and assigned students within teams. This strategy provided important scheduling advantages. It provided teachers with two conferencing times, one for planning and the other to lead an Academic Recovery Intervention (ARI). In addition, it created a way to provide interventions to struggling students that did not require pulling them out of core courses. Students at Coopersville Middle School can choose two electives each semester, but students who are identified as in need of Tier 2 support choose ARI as one elective, and then select another elective of their choosing.

Students are identified for ARI through a combination of factors including their grades, performance on the MEAP (Michigan's state assessment), the ITBS, their Reading Lexile and/or Basic Math Facts scores. During ARI, teachers work with small groups of students (teacher to student ratio of about 1:5) on a variety of skills and strategies to include writing, reading support, math tutoring, and study-skill strategies. Teachers within a team decide how best to work with students in ARI. For example, a student who is struggling in math will work with the math teacher. Students who struggle with motivation and engagement will be assigned to work with a teacher they connect with so that they can receive more individualized support as needed.

At the end of the nine-week term, student performance is reviewed. The team, together with input from the parents, decides whether intervention should be continued. After the first nine weeks of implementation, the ARI system led to a sixty percent reduction in the number of failing grades received by students selected for Tier 2. Not only has the new intervention been more effective, but the new schedule also allows Coopersville Middle School to provide the fifteen percent of struggling students with ARI support. Prior to implementing a coordinated system, the school was only able to provide intervention services to about four percent of their students and realized very few positive results (less than a one percent reduction in failing grades). Next steps for Coopersville include moving toward a blended problem-solving and standard treatment protocol approach by adopting evidence-based strategies and using Curriculum-based Measurement for progress monitoring.

Although scheduling issues are an important consideration, appropriate teacher-student ratios are critical to the success of an intervention. Many research-based interventions are effective when delivered to small groups of students, typically in a range of five to twelve. The impact of exceeding these numbers is unknown but could limit the efficacy of the intervention. Particular attention must be paid to how students are grouped and the size of the intervention groups.

Another challenge that schools face when implementing Tier 2 is providing meaningful professional development for teachers. Deshler and colleagues (2009) describe three factors that directly connect with the success of adolescents in content areas: (a) validated teacher-focused and student-focused interventions; (b) integrated and comprehensive service delivery systems; and (c) well-designed, data-based professional developmental programs. In other words, central to the success of an intervention is the provision of professional development opportunities so teachers can effectively deliver the intervention.

Finally, given the focus on developing independent learners at the secondary level, instructional strategies that prove to be beneficial for developing a Tier 2 program include both teacher-mediated and student-mediated instructional frameworks. Teacher-mediated strategy instruction is when the teacher describes, models, and provides practice (guided and independent) and constructive feedback to assist student learning and mastery of a targeted skill set with the goal of student generalization of the strategy to other content areas. Teachers scaffold student learning and actively engage students as partners in using the strategy. Cooperative learning and peer tutoring are used to provide student practice and adaptation of skills. Student-mediation of instructional strategies also includes the use of explicit instruction and modeling by the teacher, but then it is turned over to the student immediately to try out as his or her own. Peers may work together in small groups to practice and learn the strategy. Teacher- and student-mediated instruction provides a framework in which to plan, prepare, and implement targeted, research-based interventions to help students to succeed.

In Figure 6.1, interventions are targeted based on specific skill sets within the core content areas. Instruction is more explicit and

Figure 6.1   Teacher-Mediated and Student-Mediated Strategy Instruction

A Continuum of Research-Based Explicit Strategy Instruction		
	Teacher Mediated	**Student Mediated**

Reading	• Direct Instruction (DI)
	• REWARDS
	• Strategic Instruction Model (SIM)
	   o Word Identification
	   o Visual Imagery
	   o Self-Questioning
	   o Paraphrasing
	   o Inference
	   o Word Mapping
		• Reciprocal Teaching
		• Peer-Assisted Learning Strategies (PALS)
		• Transactional Strategy Instruction (TSI)
		• Collaborative Strategic Reading (CSR)
		• Question the Author

Writing	• Self-Regulated Strategy Development (SRSD)
	• SIM
	   o Sentence Writing
	   o Paragraph Writing
	   o Error Monitoring
	   o Paraphrasing and Summarizing
		• PALS
		• Write to Learn
		• 6 + 1 Trait Writing

Math	• Concrete-Representational-Abstract Sequence (CRA) • Schema-Based Word Problem Solving • SOLVE IT Strategy	• PALS • Problem-Solving Process • Inquiry and Exploration

Affective	• ASSET: A Social Skills Curriculum for Adolescents
	• Walker Social Skills: The ACCEPTS Program
	• The PREPARE Curriculum: Teaching Prosocial Competencies
	• CHAMPs: A Proactive and Positive Approach to Classroom Management
		• Peer Tutoring
		• Cooperative Learning
		• SIM
		   o Possible Selves: Nurturing Student Motivation
		   o SCORE Skills: Social Skills for Cooperative Groups
		   o Community Building and Learning Series

Study/ Organization Skills	• Mnemonic/Keyword Strategies
	• SIM
	   o Test Taking
	   o Essay Test Taking
	   o Assignment Completion
		• Peer Tutoring
		• Cooperative Learning

intensive in nature with teacher mediation that evolves into student facilitation and independent use of targeted strategies. Often, a strategy that begins as a teacher-mediated approach will move into student-mediated instruction as the students make the strategy their own and generalizes its use.

The purpose for which a teacher uses a strategy will determine how it will be taught in class. Often, instructional strategies can be employed as "teaching tools" or "learning tools" depending upon their intended use (Conley, 2008). For example, when teachers decide to use a graphic organizer to convey critical content to the class, the organizer becomes a vehicle to impart knowledge in an organized fashion to the class. In this instance, the graphic organizer is a teaching tool. However, if the goal is to develop the analytical and reasoning skills of students, then the graphic organizer becomes a learning tool that a student can use to assist with the development and processing of information. In this case, the students are explicitly taught how to use the organizer to create their own mental model to organize information and support their thinking.

Traditionally, instruction in the content areas is delivered in isolation without much conversation or feedback from colleagues. This practice has created classrooms of "siloed" instruction. That is, instruction that is not informed or carried out in collaboration with peers. In many cases, collaboration is thought to just happen; however, it must be encouraged and fostered so that it may develop and form over time. Teachers must feel confident to share their expertise with others. One way to bring about teacher confidence and expertise for using newly adopted research-based interventions is to provide meaningful professional development opportunities that supports and aligns with the goals stated in the school improvement plan. Tier 2 teachers and specialists must be well-versed and prepared in the delivery of strategy-based instruction that is generalized to core content and reinforced in general education.

So, after assessing students and making data-driven decisions, instructional strategies and practices need to be selected and implemented. When choosing research-based instructional strategies and programs, the current academic and support programs provided must be reviewed based on how well they support student performance. In addition, these newly selected techniques must be supported by a school infrastructure that is conducive to student learning. Thinking outside of the box and having flexibility in scheduling and structuring curriculum courses to meet the skill specific and targeted needs of students who require intervention at Tier 2 will be critical for success.

4. *Do we have a clearly defined, schoolwide set of behavioral expectations and a system to support student engagement?* Having a clearly defined set of expectations for student behavior, as defined in Tier 1, is essential for the successful implementation of RTI. However, intervention at Tier 2 for secondary schools must move beyond establishing a common set of student expectations and providing a fair and consistent process to handle behavior issues. Behavior interventions at secondary school levels must also include the development of school culture conducive to promoting student engagement and a curriculum that provides effective transition supports as students progress through grade levels.

Engagement and motivation are serious concerns at the secondary levels. So, how can the number of students who are at risk for failing and eventually dropping out of school be addressed and remedied? First, these students must be identified, and then the supports and programs necessary to tackle these needs can be implemented. Heppen and Therriault (2008) indicate two key warning signs that students are at risk of dropping out of school: continued academic failure and absenteeism. Tracking student progress, especially during the first year of high school, can help to indicate future success. For example, students who earn at least five credit hours and do not fail more than one class during their freshman year are more likely to graduate (Heppen & Therriault, 2008). In addition, those students who miss more than one to two weeks of school during the first semester are at tremendous risk of failing the ninth grade. Therefore, schools must develop a system for "flagging" those students who are not on track to graduate based on their academic performance and attendance during their freshman year in high school (Jerald, 2007).

Next, given the importance of making sure that students are on the right path to success during the first year of high school, schools must examine the question: What are the best practices for initiating and sustaining student retention rates at the secondary level? Engaging students in learning and helping them to see the relevance of a high school education is imperative. Teachers, administrators, and support staff can create a school culture that provides a sense of belonging and is inclusive for all students. For those students who have been identified as not "on track" to graduate, providing adult and/or peer mentoring can be a powerful way to connect with and support these students. Kennelly and Monrad (2007) provide specific areas schools can address to affect student engagement at the secondary levels: (a) school climate, (b) academic rigor, (c) effective teaching, and (d) extended learning time. By establishing approaches and making adjustments to the programs in place, schools can take charge and provide the conditions that encourage student success. Thus, schools must evaluate where they are in the process by determining which practices will address the needs of students who struggle and face a variety of challenges in and out of the classroom.

To further assist with engaging students at the secondary level, Ascher, Henderson, and Maguire (2008) suggest four indicators of good practice to help students to "beat the odds" despite having academic difficulties and environmental obstacles. These key components are as follows: (1) academic rigor, (2) network of timely supports, (3) culture of college access, and (4) effective use of data. Focusing attention on these four components, Ascher and colleagues developed a rubric for schools to use to evaluate how well they are preparing students who are college ready (for more information on the College Pathways Rubric, please go to http://www.annenberg institute.org).

As previously mentioned, by the time students who have struggled and found little or no success in school reach the secondary level, many are apathetic and feel that school has very little to offer them with respect to achieving future aspirations. Developing programs that address student motivation and self-esteem as well as the exploration of career interests and life goals is very important. Therefore, Tier 2 programming should include interventions that address motivational and goal-setting strategies as well as approaches for how to build learning communities. For example, Possible Selves (Hock, Schumaker, & Deshler, 2001) is a strategy that increases student motivation by exploring strengths and weaknesses, hopes and fears, and setting realistic goals for the future. Teachers lead students through several lessons with activities that focus student attention on goal setting, self-regulation, and self-reflection. In addition, implementing a curriculum that encourages community building and learning will greatly benefit those students who need additional behavioral supports above and beyond the universal positive behavior support provided at Tier 1.

In addition to implementing programs that promote self-awareness and discovery, schools must examine how they can better provide additional supports that help students to transition through the grade levels and into postsecondary education and employment opportunities. The development of such programs will increase the likelihood of student success by facilitating seamless transitions for students as they move between school buildings and progress through grade levels (Ascher, Henderson, & Maguire, 2008). Developing programs to support students who need to explore postsecondary education options and employment opportunities as they transition through the grade levels is vital to the success of those who struggle, are at risk for failure, or on a path to dropping out of school (Kennelly & Monrad, 2007).

Furthermore, establishing before- and after-school programs is beneficial to all students. However, providing additional initiatives such as peer tutoring, mentoring, or coaching programs increases the likelihood of success of troubled students. Additional supports that include comprehensive and wrap-around services can make a positive difference in the lives of students struggling to complete high school (Kennelly & Monrad, 2007).

Once these questions have been addressed, the team can begin to develop a quality Tier 2 program and curriculum guided by student data. The following is an account of Tier 2 implementation at Mattawan High School to increase the performance and meet the instructional needs of its students who struggle in Tier 1.

TIER 2 IN PRACTICE: MATTAWAN HIGH SCHOOL

Mattawan High School began the process of RTI implementation in the 2007–2008 academic year. This included an initiative to provide academic and behavioral supports for all students and professional development opportunities and learning communities for teachers. The primary goal is to provide and guarantee a curriculum aligned to the High School Content Expectations (HSCE) for all students. The principal organized a leadership team, the Faculty Advisory Council (FAC), to develop a schoolwide plan to improve reading and writing outcomes for all students, and focus on programming that would help students earn graduation credit. The belief system is that all students can learn at grade level; failure is not an option. The FAC was primarily interested in developing an intervention program to support the approximately fifteen percent of their students who were struggling with completing their schoolwork and were at risk for failing courses.

Mattawan collected data on all students in the following areas: attendance, behavior, and academic achievement. As students transition into the ninth grade, they are given the ACT EXPLORE (college and career readiness test). The FAC uses the results of these assessments and recommendations by teachers from middle school regarding student attendance, behavior, and basic skills to determine which students require interventions.

Because the staff at Mattawan believed strongly that all students should be supported to learn and achieve at grade level, the staff decided to use strategy instruction as the main approach to designing Tier 2 interventions. Within this structure, a student service team consisting of school counselors, administrators, and social workers work with struggling students. Recognizing that the intensity of student needs will vary,

Mattawan developed a "pyramid of interventions." The pyramid of interventions is a "levels within tiers" system that includes five levels within a three-tiered system. The five levels fit within a tertiary RTI model and were developed using the Content Literacy Continuum (CLC) framework as a guide (see the Resources for more information on the CLC framework). Tiers 1 and 2 each contain two levels, followed by Tier 3, which consists of intensive language programming and, depending on student need, leads to special education services. Mattawan found that within the three tiers, different types and varying levels of support were needed to better service all students, especially in Tiers 1 and 2. The levels within Tier 1 infuse differentiated instruction, embed strategy instruction, make accommodations, and provide after-school support to meet student needs. Tier 2 increases the intensity of instruction delivered in each level by explicitly teaching learning strategies, allotting additional time on targeted skills, providing generous practice with application and generalization to core content, and providing after-school programs and support. Within the framework of the CLC, Mattawan instituted the use and implementation of the Strategic Instructional Model (SIM) to address how to deliver the instruction of research-based interventions and which ones to use.

To facilitate Tier 2 implementation, Mattawan High made several changes to the existing school structure. Tier 2 includes course programming called "double blocks" and after-school programs. Double-block courses consist of adding additional time (approximately sixty minutes) to a targeted area by putting two periods together for a total of one hundred and twenty minutes. Students who are identified as needing Tier 2 support choose block courses as one elective, and then select another elective of their choosing; students give up one elective course to be in block classes. This system created a way to provide interventions to struggling students that did not require pulling them out of core courses.

In addition to the supports afforded to students during school, an after-school program was started. The Core Academic Tutorial Service (CATS) is offered three nights a week so that students can take tests, make up missed assignments, and complete homework. Students are given time to make up work and time in class. Volunteers, including teachers and parents, are available to assist students in homework completion. The students who typically attend the afterschool sessions are those who benefit from Tier 2 intervention and truly need the additional support. Since instituting this program, the number of students who receive failing grades has been decreasing.

Mattawan is still in the beginning stages of developing a comprehensive RTI model that meets the needs of all students who attend. During these early stages, Mattawan has developed a vision and belief that all students can learn, reorganized school infrastructure and programming based on student data, and provided meaningful teacher development opportunities to better serve the instructional needs of their students.

TIER 3 IMPLEMENTATION

It is beyond the scope of this text to discuss quality special education programming for students at the secondary level. However, there are key factors to consider when implementing Tier 3 within an RTI framework. Tier 3 services are quite likely already in place in most secondary schools. Because schools are required to provide special education services to students with disabilities, there is probably a system for providing individualized supports and specially designed instruction to help students meet individualized goals aligned with the general curriculum. The key to successful Tier 3 services is that they are integrated and supportive of progress in Tier 1.

LEADER TASKS

For many principals, Tiers 2 and 3 represent the most challenging component of RTI implementation. An implementation checklist for Tiers 2 and 3 is included in the Appendix. Schools have to decide how best to approach assisting those students who teeter on the brink of failure and lack the skills necessary to be successful in the general education setting. Hence, focusing on this group is a reasonable place to begin to make changes that can increase student overall academic and behavioral performance. However, the intervention provided in Tiers 2 and 3 also requires the greatest coordination of resources. For successful implementation, principals will need to do the following:

1. Support the selection and adoption of data-driven programs to deliver more intensive, small-group instruction to support students who struggle in Tier 1.

2. Provide and coordinate professional development opportunities.

3. Develop an infrastructure that allows for collaboration among teachers and the scheduling of Tier 2 interventions.

4. Develop academic and behavior programs that support area(s) of deficit and monitor student progress in the general curriculum.

5. Create a system for establishing parent communication and family involvement.

SUMMARY

A tiered system of intervention can provide needed supports to struggling students. A primary purpose of Tier 2 is to provide additional support with targeted interventions to students who struggle in Tier 1. Tier 2 is the proverbial "safety net" for those students who need explicit and intensive strategy instruction to be successful in the general education setting. Establishing a quality program at this level is contingent on the quality of professional development received by teachers and requires decisions based on student needs, targeted strategy instruction, and continuous monitoring of student achievement. Quality Tier 3 programming is essential to meet the needs of secondary students with disabilities. Tier 3 programming should be aligned as much as possible with the Tier 1 program. Continuous collaboration and communication among administration, teachers, and parents across all tiers is vital and will lead to improved student outcomes.

7

Progress Monitoring

DEFINITION: WHAT IS PROGRESS MONITORING?

Progress monitoring is the routine assessment of student performance to determine whether the student is responding adequately to the instructional program. In an RTI framework, progress monitoring is conducted at all tiers of instruction. Progress monitoring provides information at the individual student level, the classroom level, and the school level. Based on the data provided by progress-monitoring measures, teachers can determine the efficacy of the overall program and determine individual student response to the instruction or intervention (Fuchs & Fuchs, 2006). Progress monitoring offers many benefits to teachers and their students. A recent review of research indicates that when implemented correctly, progress monitoring provides the following:

1. Documentation of student progress for accountability purposes.

2. Better informed instructional and intervention decisions.

3. Higher expectations for students.

4. Improved outcomes for students. (Stecker, Fuchs, & Fuchs, 2005)

Different types of assessments frequently associated with progress monitoring include Curriculum-based Measurement (CBM), Curriculum-based Assessment (CBA), and Mastery Measurement (Fuchs, 2007). Of these, CBM is the form of assessment that allows for the measurement of growth across the curriculum. CBA and mastery measurement do not allow for the measurement of growth across a content area, but they do play an important role in a tiered assessment and instruction system. In this chapter, we offer definitions of each of these forms of assessment, discuss the purpose of progress monitoring at the secondary level, and describe how progress monitoring can be implemented at each tier. Case stories drawn from school-based experiences show examples of how progress monitoring has been used at the secondary level.

Mastery measurement is a type of assessment typically used by teachers and involves the assessment of a series of short-term instructional objectives. In employing mastery measurement, the teacher determines a sensible instructional sequence for the school year and designs criterion-referenced testing procedures to match each step in that instructional sequence (U.S. Department of Education [USDE], 2002). For example, in math, a teacher might create a skill hierarchy for multiplication that includes skip counting (e.g., counting by twos, counting by fives), multiplying one digit by one digit (e.g., $2 \times 2 = 4$), missing factor multiplication (e.g., $2 \times \_\_ = 8$), and then multiplying a two-digit number by a one-digit number with no regrouping (e.g., 21×3) (Stein, Kinder, Silbert, & Carnine, 2006). Mastery measurement determines whether a student has successfully completed each specific skill before he or she moves on to the next one. Mastery measurement also provides a system to sequence instruction. For example, in social studies, teachers may decide it is important for students to learn about the Revolutionary War before teaching about the U.S. Civil War. One core principle of mastery measurement is that students should not move on to the next skill until they have "mastered" the current skill (USDE, 2002). This limits its use as a monitoring tool because mastery measurement does not depict growth across the curriculum; it only measures growth for a specific skill within that curriculum (Fuchs, 2007).

The term Curriculum-based Assessment, or CBA, was coined by Gickling and Havertape (1981) to refer to "assessment practices in which the instructional needs of students were determined by measuring the ratio of known to unknown material in the curriculum" (Salvia, Ysseldyke, & Bolt, 2006). The goal of most CBA is to match instruction to the student's current level of skills (Shapiro, 2004). For example, to determine an appropriate reading level for students, students may be given a grade-level reading passage and asked to read for one minute. In addition to determining the words correct per minute, a teacher also will evaluate the number of errors the student made to identify three levels of instructional match: frustration level, instructional level, and independent level (Shapiro, 2004). In the content areas, the use of common assessments reflects a form of CBA, especially when used as both a pre- and posttest to determine instructional groupings. CBA requires the use of curriculum-based probes that broadly reflect the various skills students should master.

Curriculum-based Measurement, or CBM, refers to a set of procedures for measuring student growth in basic skills that was developed by Deno

(1985). CBM differs from other forms of CBA in a number of important ways (Fuchs & Deno, 1991). CBM focuses on long-term goals, such as the development of strong reading proficiency, rather than on short-term goals, such as determining whether a student comprehended a specific story. CBM uses a standardized set of measures that represent a broad sample of the skills students are expected to master within a content area (Hintze & Silberglitt, 2005). When the student completes several CBM measures over time, CBM allows for the assessment of individual student progress and growth (Hintze & Silberglitt, 2005) as well as for the comparison of student performance across grade levels. In addition, the routine use of CBM for students with learning difficulties can provide immediate feedback on student progress that informs instructional planning (Fletcher, Lyon, Fuchs, & Barnes, 2007). An extensive research base on CBM supports its use as a progress-monitoring tool to raise student achievement and inform instructional decision making (Stecker & Lembke, 2005).

In summary, although CBM is the form of assessment that provides information about student response to instruction, CBA and mastery measurement processes play important roles in a comprehensive assessment system to determine student performance in an RTI framework. As explained in the following section, each form of assessment has a unique role in determining student performance and growth at the various instructional tiers.

PURPOSE OF PROGRESS MONITORING AT THE SECONDARY LEVEL

The purpose of progress monitoring at the secondary level depends upon the tier of intervention. Table 7.1 summarizes the purposes and types of assessments used at the different tiers. In the general education program (Tier 1), progress monitoring allows teachers to see whether all students are achieving at expected grade-level performance benchmarks. This information, when reviewed across classrooms within a grade level, also provides a common system through which teachers can compare student performance, align their curriculum, and evaluate their students' performance. In this way, building level leaders can help ensure more consistency of instruction across classrooms and use the feedback to target professional development needs. At Tier 2, progress monitoring is used to determine both the short- and long-term outcomes of academic interventions, primarily through the use of CBM. The short-term outcomes are monitored to determine whether an intervention is working for an individual student or whether adjustments need to be made to the student's program. Long-term outcomes are monitored to determine overall program efficacy—is the intervention effective in supporting

| Table 7.1 | Purpose and Type of Progress Monitoring Used at Different Tiers |

	Purpose of Progress Monitoring	*Type of Progress Monitoring*
Tier 1	• Determine whether all students are meeting content area benchmarks • Horizontal alignment of curriculum	CBA—Common Assessments Mastery Measurement
Tier 2	• Inform intervention decisions • Monitor student growth in interventions • Determine long-term efficacy of interventions	CBM
Tier 3	• Monitor progress toward individual IEP goals	CBM Mastery Measurement

students' attainment of grade-level performance benchmarks? For progress monitoring to answer these questions, the measures must be direct, must be repeated, and must incorporate a time series analysis (graphing/visual display of the progress overtime) (Shapiro, 2004). At Tier 3, progress monitoring is used to determine student progress toward Individualized Education Plan (IEP) goals.

IMPLEMENTATION

Schools have access to numerous resources to facilitate adoption, implementation, and maintenance of progress-monitoring systems. At the time of this writing, two national centers, the Research Institute on Progress Monitoring (http://www.progressmonitoring.net) and the National Center on Student Progress Monitoring (http://www.studentprogress.org), provide materials, research briefs, webinars, and online tools to help schools select tools and resources, particularly CBM progress-monitoring tools. Nevertheless, establishing effective schoolwide progress-monitoring procedures requires strong leadership to develop the necessary infrastructure. The success of RTI requires systematic assessment and progress monitoring at all tiers. Figure 7.1 shows how progress monitoring works across tiers to provide both individual student- and systems-level data that can inform instructional planning. More information for how to implement progress monitoring in each tier follows.

Figure 7.1   How Progress Monitoring Works Across Tiers

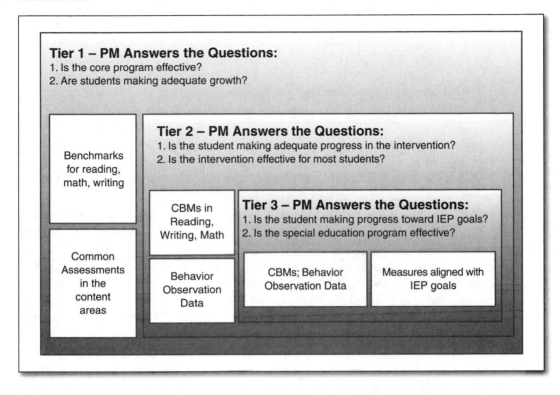

Tier 1

At Tier 1, it is important to identify which students are meeting performance-level benchmarks and whether they are placed in the appropriate instructional level. Although benchmarking is not progress monitoring, benchmarking is necessary in Tier 1 to identify students who, without further intervention and support, will not be successful. At the classroom, grade, and school levels, this process also allows schools to monitor their growth in supporting student achievement. For example, after research-based instructional practices are implemented in Tier 1 (see Chapter 5), a school should witness increased numbers of students meeting established performance benchmarks. Benchmark data can be collected across the curriculum. For ease of discussion, we have separated progress monitoring in Tier 1 into two sections (a) progress monitoring of the core academic skills and (b) progress monitoring in the content areas.

Progress monitoring in reading, writing, and math

Progress monitoring in the core academic skills provides important information about a school's performance. Because reading, writing, and math are considered foundational not only to success within school, but also for postsecondary school success, it is critical to routinely assess the performance of students in these areas. The number of available tools to monitor progress continues to grow at a rapid pace, so the web-based resources provided in this text should be periodically checked for new information. The screening measures (see Chapter 4) that are administered in fall, winter, and spring also provide information on student progress across these areas.

Progress monitoring in the content areas

Mastery measurement and CBA are the most commonly used assessments in the content areas at Tier 1. Increasingly, schools are moving toward the use of a form of CBA also known as common assessments. Common assessments, typically consisting of twenty to twenty-five questions, are developed, administered, and systematically reviewed by all teachers across a specific content and grade level (e.g., all sixth-grade science teachers) (McTighe & Emberger, 2006). They also are aligned with "power standards" that focus the curriculum (Marzano, 2003). Power standards are those identified by teachers as the most important within a content area that enable teachers to focus curriculum and instruction for students. All students in the same grade take the common assessment at the same time. Teachers then conduct an item analysis to evaluate student performance. For common assessments to work effectively, the curriculum must be aligned horizontally. That is, all content teachers at a specific grade level must teach the same material at the same time. Fisher and Johnson (2006) offer a protocol for developing common assessments:

1. Develop instructional pacing guides. Teachers decide on a timeline for the sequence of instruction so that all teachers are addressing the same content at a given time.

2. Select common instructional materials and strategies. When teachers use common instructional materials and similar strategies, there is a greater probability that the selected content and performance standards will be addressed equally in all classrooms. This limits the impact of "classroom effects" on student performance.

3. Develop (or select) and administer common assessments. Many curriculum companies are beginning to include unit assessments that can serve either as common assessments or as a good starting point for developing common assessments. The team of content and grade-level teachers needs to review assessments to ensure alignment with the selected content standards. Then, at predetermined times in the school year, but no less often than every six weeks, teachers administer the common assessments to all students.

4. Score assessments by consensus and conduct an item analysis. Once all of the students have participated in the common assessment, teachers meet to discuss the results. The results are presented for the grade level or the course at this meeting, not for individual teachers, though individual teachers will want to review their class performance at a later time. Item analysis consists of reviewing the responses to each particular item to determine overall performance. This type of review can indicate whether teachers need to focus instruction on a particular skill or subject. The review also can help teachers identify items that may need revision. In addition, results should be disaggregated by significant subpopulations, such as students with disabilities and students who are learning English, to determine how well the instructional program supports their learning.

5. Revise pacing guides and assessments as needed. Reteach and consider intervention groups for students whose performance is of concern.

Determining response to Tier 1 instruction

The purpose of progress monitoring at any tier is to determine student response to the instruction or intervention. How is adequate response defined at Tier 1? Content and performance standards that guide the curriculum provide a helpful starting point for developing common assessments and determining adequate response. When teams review grade-level results, high percentages of students from one class who are not successful on a particular item indicate that the teacher may need to reteach that concept. When only small numbers of students are not successful, those students may require additional support to acquire the content knowledge or skill. National, state, or local norms can be used to compare student performance in areas of reading, math, and writing. For example, AIMSweb publishes norms for performance on oral reading fluency, maze (a reading measure), math, and writing probes for grades K–12 and includes a breakdown by percentile rank. An RTI team may set a goal of reviewing the work of students whose performance falls at the thirtieth percentile or below on these measures. At the initial stages of implementation, national norms may be used as a starting point until sufficient data are collected to provide stable local norms.

Tier 1 progress monitoring in practice

Common assessments can be developed across the content areas. Figure 7.2 is an example of a common assessment in social studies that is used by the staff at Cheyenne Mountain Junior High School. All students complete the assessment that includes writing an essay in which they

Figure 7.2	Social Studies Common Assessment From Cheyenne Mountain Junior High

Our Living Constitution

Civics Standard 1.3: Students understand the principles of the United States constitutional government.

Students can develop and defend positions on current issues involving constitutional protection of individual rights.

Directions: You will develop a packet that includes articles and short essays as described in the rubric below. For each constitutional principle and amendment (total of 6) you will find one news article about a recent court case, issue, editorial, or current event for the constitutional principles and constitutional amendments listed below. Summarize each article and explain how the events in the article apply to that protected right in a short essay.

Section 1

Pick the following three constitutional principles.

   a. Federalism—The states and national government share powers.
   b. Checks and Balances—Each branch of government can exercise checks and controls over the other branches.
   c. Limited Government—The power of the government is limited.

Section 2

Complete the first and fourteenth constitutional amendments. Then, pick one additional amendment listed in C (4, 5, 6, or 8).

   a. Amendment 1—Freedom of religion, speech, press, assembly, or petition government.
   b. Amendment 14—Provides equal protection of the law for all citizens.
   c. Amendment 4, 5, 6, or 8—Right to privacy, criminal due process, and protection from cruel and unusual punishment.

develop and defend positions on current issues involving the constitutional protection of individual rights. Once complete, teachers use a common rubric to evaluate student work, identify gaps in learning, and plan instructional changes as needed.

Common assessments are used in the content areas. To assess routine performance and growth in reading, math, and writing at Tier 1, Cheyenne Mountain uses the *Performance Series* CBMs to monitor student progress (see the Resources). Within Tier 1 at the secondary level, CBMs are given only three times per year (fall, winter, and spring) and are used as both a progress-monitoring tool (e.g., Are students showing consistent growth from one benchmark to the next?) and as a component of a screening process (e.g., students who do not meet benchmarks may be considered for further assessment and intervention).

Tier 2

In Tier 2, progress monitoring can be used to determine both short- and long-term outcomes of academic interventions (Shapiro, 2004). Students who receive interventions in the basic skills areas such as reading, writing, or math will require frequent (e.g., weekly) monitoring (Espin & Tindal, 1999). CBM is most frequently used for this purpose. However, the research on CBM at the secondary level indicates that the measures that are used at the elementary level are not necessarily appropriate for use at the secondary school level (Espin & Tindal, 1999). The Research Institute on Progress Monitoring (RIPM) recommends using the following types of measures in reading, writing, and math (RIPM, n.d.):

Reading

To monitor progress in reading at the secondary level, a maze procedure has been shown to have better reliability and validity for measuring student growth than the use of ORF (RIPM, n.d.). A maze is a passage in which every seventh or tenth word is deleted and replaced with three choices from which a student must select the correct word (see Figure 7.3 for a sample maze passage). Students are given three minutes to read the passage and circle the correct multiple-choice item for each blank they encounter. Although oral reading fluency passages are available at the secondary level, research has indicated that maze measures produce more reliable growth rates than reading aloud (Espin & Foegen, 1996). Procedures for developing a maze passage are found in Espin and Foegen (1996).

Oral reading fluency (ORF) measures are now more widely available for secondary levels (see the Resources for more information). ORF measures are passages organized by grade level. Students are typically given one minute to read the passage aloud, and the number of words correctly

Figure 7.3   Sample Maze Passage

Only one guard stood on duty when Brown and his small army marched into town; the guard thought the men were playing some kind of joke. When he saw rifles pointed in _____ direction,
(girl, his, black)
he knew differently. He was _____ a prisoner, and John Brown and _____ followers controlled
(soon, bear, jump)   (but, see, his)
the armory. Then a _____ came by. Disciplined soldiers might have _____ calmly, but Brown's
(white, train, learn)   (shark, brown, acted)
men panicked and _____ an innocent railroad worker (who happened _____ be black, and free).
(killed, truck, person)   (in, as, to)
After that, ____ let the railroad cars go on ___ way. That was foolish. The people ___ the train
(fish, low, they)   (their, down, fort)   (is, on, do)
took news of the _____ to Washington and Baltimore. (excerpt taken from Hakim (1999), p. 55)
(uprising, purple, jumped)

read within one minute is counted. Some of the advantages of ORF over maze include that a teacher can listen to the student read. In this way, in addition to getting a count of the words read correctly, the teacher is also provided with more insight on the student's abilities. ORF tends to have higher "face validity" then maze. Some advantages of maze over ORF aside from those mentioned above include that it can be group administered.

Writing

The research on progress monitoring in writing suggests that one promising measure is the use of a writing prompt followed by five minutes of student writing and scored by counting the number of correct minus the number of incorrect word sequences (Espin et al., 2000). This progress-monitoring tool is recommended only for use with students who have severe discrepancies in their writing ability, in part because of the time-consuming nature of scoring (teachers must hand-score assessments) and in part because although this measure has been shown to reliably discriminate between groups of good and poor writers, its use as a reliable measure of growth for all students has not been adequately demonstrated. Writing progress also can be monitored through counting total words written (TWW), which simply counts the total number of words (correctly spelled or not) a student produces in the allotted time. TWW provides a reliable indication of student growth, but teachers must be careful not to encourage students simply to write *more* words as a way to increase their performance (Shinn, 2005). Written Expression CBM (WE-CBM) also includes a qualitative checklist and a running record of errors (Shinn, 2005) that can be helpful for teachers analyzing student performance over time and using WE-CBM for instructional programming decisions.

Content areas

In content-area learning, one promising CBM is the use of a vocabulary matching procedure (Espin, Busch, Shin & Kruschwitz, 2001). This procedure measures student progress using vocabulary assessments consisting of twenty items randomly selected from the entire list of the subject's vocabulary terms for that grade level. The assessments give a brief definition for each term as well as two distracter definitions, and students have five minutes to complete the vocabulary-matching measure (Busch & Espin, 2003; Espin et al., 2001).

Vocabulary matching has been demonstrated to be a strong predictor of student performance and growth in the content areas (Espin et al., 2001), but unlike the standardized measures developed in reading, writing, and math, there are no standard measures for vocabulary, nor are there norms for rates of improvement as there are for reading and math. That means that at the present time, teachers have to construct vocabulary measures for use as monitoring tools. In small implementation studies, the process of constructing assessments was greatly assisted through electronic versions of vocabulary lists (either from state assessments or curriculum guides). These lists were entered into a database, along with a short definition, and items to form random lists were selected (Johnson, Greenlee, & Brown, 2009). The construction of these assessments led intervention teachers to focus vocabulary instruction to support student participation in the general education science class (Johnson et al., 2009).

Math

In recent years, several mathematics progress-monitoring tools for secondary levels have been developed (see the Resources). These tools monitor progress in a variety of mathematical areas, including computation, measures of algebra, and problem solving. Computation and applied problem probes through grade 12 are readily available from a variety of sources. At the middle school level, estimation tasks have been shown to be effective indicators of student progress (Lembke & Stecker, 2007). Estimation tasks involve multiple-choice assessments consisting of computation or word problems administered for three minutes. Students circle their best estimate of the answer. At the high school level, measures related to algebra have been shown to be robust indicators of performance, especially those that include standard algebra skills such as graphing slope and intercept or evaluating equations (Foegen, Olson, & Impecoven-Lind, 2008).

Determining response to Tier 2 intervention

An important component in using CBM to determine student progress is the visual display of performance overtime. This is usually done by plotting student scores on a graph (see Figure 7.4). To graph student performance, several steps are required (adapted from Stecker & Lembke, 2005):

1. Collect a baseline of three to five scores for the student.

2. Using the median baseline score, determine an appropriate goal for the student. Goals should forecast out a number of weeks—recommended guidelines are from nine to twelve weeks for Tier 2 (Vaughn, 2003). Goals can be set by using published rate of improvement (ROI) norms, or by using established benchmarks. See Stecker and Lembke (2005) for a detailed description of how to determine appropriate goals. Once a goal is determined, plot the goal at the appropriate week on the graph, and draw a goal line from the median baseline score to the goal.

3. Collect student data by administering and plotting weekly performance. Most commercial programs will draw a trend line and indicate whether student performance is on track for meeting the goal, whether the goal needs to be raised, or whether the student is not making sufficient progress and an instructional change is required. For schools that do not have the resources to use a commercial program, helpful resources such as a template for graphing CBM results are available on Jim Wright's Intervention Central website, http://www.interventioncentral.org.

The graph in Figure 7.4 displays an eighth-grade student's baseline, goal, and trend line in reading as measured by a maze CBM procedure. The student's baseline score is 10. Based on norms for eighth-grade performance, a score of 10 in the fall places the student in the tenth percentile (Hosp, Hosp, & Howell, 2007). By spring, we hope to have the student performing at the twenty-fifth percentile or better—this would give a goal of between seventeen to thirty-one words correctly restored (Hosp et al., 2007). We continue to collect data on this student's performance and plot it. As the graph illustrates, this student is making adequate progress toward his goal. Based on the data collected to date, the intervention should be continued as currently implemented.

Figure 7.4   CBM Graph

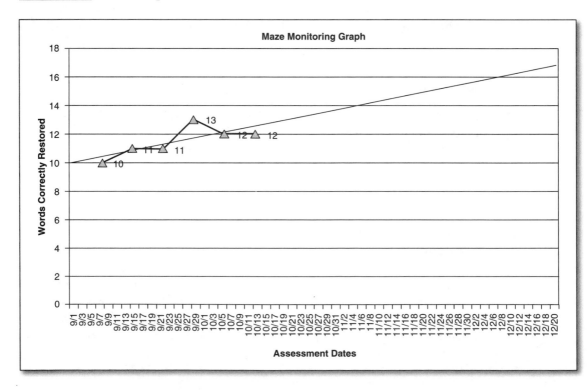

Tier 3

The use of CBM probes for frequent progress monitoring has been demonstrated to be an effective means of improving outcomes for students with disabilities. Goals for students receiving special education services may require an individualized approach depending on the current level of performance of the student. Alternatively, teachers may find they need to administer CBM probes below the student's grade-level placement in order to obtain a reliable measure of growth. Grade-level probes should still be collected periodically to provide a comparison of the student's performance relative to grade-level peers. The frequency of progress monitoring at Tier 3 also increases, with recommendations varying from daily to twice weekly (Stecker & Lembke, 2005). The frequent collection and analysis of data provide feedback to teachers so that they may make instructional adjustments for individual students. In addition, at Tier 3, special education teachers may rely on mastery measurement approaches for skills that cannot be assessed through CBM. For example, students with transition plans may need to work on developing skills that will make them successful in the workplace, and these would likely best be measured through the use of task analyses and related mastery measurement tools.

Determining response to Tier 3 instruction

At Tier 3, a number of strategies can be used to determine student response to instruction. Goals for student performance should be clearly stated in the student's IEP. If CBM probes are used to monitor progress, the same process as described in Tier 2 is used to graph and evaluate student performance; however, goals will be based on the student's level of performance, and the special education teacher may need to monitor progress using grade-level measures below the student's current grade placement. Goals that are measured using a mastery measurement or CBA approach should be written in clear, objective, and measurable terms, to include the criteria and condition under which the performance is evaluated. For example, a clear, objective, and measurable goal related to a student's job performance—arriving to the job on time—might be written as "Given a bus schedule and pass, the student will have no more than four late arrivals to his job site each month." Then, the student, the job site manager, and the teacher will record the student's arrival each day, and progress toward the goal can be measured.

LEADER TASKS

Progress monitoring lies at the heart of the RTI process, because it is the use of formative assessment, or assessment *for* learning (Stiggins, 2002) that provides teachers with the feedback they need to adjust instruction or interventions to support student learning. To establish progress monitoring schoolwide, strong planning is required on the part of the building leader. Creating a systemic approach to progress monitoring is crucial to the success of the RTI process, and it will demand the greatest amount of time and resources for initial implementation. Building leaders will need to do the following:

1. Assign collaborative teams to develop common assessments for use in the Tier 1 setting.

2. Provide logistical and administrative support, including planning and meeting time, access to standards and other frameworks to guide the assessment development process, and planning for times to review and evaluate performance.

3. For schools implementing CBM models of progress monitoring, select existing tools or procedures and plan for professional development needs.

4. Coordinate times and processes for analyzing and evaluating data that have been collected.

5. Decide who will be the "data person" for the building—the person who has the responsibility for collecting data. Many secondary schools designate counselors or school psychologists to fulfill this role.

SUMMARY

Progress monitoring serves an important function in an RTI model. Decades of research on formative assessment and CBM procedures have documented that when teachers routinely measure student progress, evaluate the results, and make instructional changes when needed, their students achieve higher outcomes than the students of teachers who do not (Deno, 2001; Fuchs, Deno, & Mirkin, 1984; Stecker, Fuchs, & Fuchs, 2005). In essence, progress monitoring indicates the "response" within the RTI framework. When implemented schoolwide with rigor, progress monitoring allows a school to identify students who require additional interventions and allows staff to determine whether a given intervention is successful.

8

Conclusion

Response to Intervention is a framework that is expected to lead to better teaching and learning. Unlike other educational initiatives, RTI provides an umbrella under which numerous research-based practices can be brought to bear to improve student learning. Throughout this text, we have discussed the purpose of RTI at the secondary level and offered resources for and descriptions of the various RTI components. In this final chapter, we summarize how RTI is expected to lead to improved student learning, re-emphasize the critical role of strong school leadership to make RTI a success, and provide two case stories of implementation that explain why we are optimistic about the future of RTI as an effective framework to improve student learning.

HOW IS RTI EXPECTED TO LEAD TO IMPROVED STUDENT LEARNING?

Deno and Mirkin (1977) provided the blueprint for modern-day RTI in their work *Data-based Program Modification*. In this document, they carefully detail how a DBDM process aligned with instructional practices that are known to be effective for students with learning disabilities can result in improved instructional planning and student outcomes. The term RTI evolved from their work over the years and now includes the use of Curriculum-based Measurement (CBM), also developed by Deno and colleagues and further refined by the Research Institute on Progress Monitoring at the University of Minnesota and the

National Center on Student Progress Monitoring at the American Institutes for Research and Vanderbilt University. Nearly three decades of research supports the contention that when teachers routinely assess student response to the instructional program and environment, student achievement improves.

The RTI framework has since expanded to apply to all grade levels (K–12) and across all content areas. Under the umbrella of RTI, especially when it is used as a means of building capacity to better serve the needs of all students, numerous research-based practices can be integrated to lead to continuous school improvement. This includes evidenced-based practices for curriculum, instruction, and assessment. In addition, given the focus of RTI on determining individual response to instruction, teachers must not only be content matter experts but also must learn how to deliver instruction in ways that meet the needs of a diverse student population.

Because RTI stems from the preventive sciences, in which effective instruction and early intervention are seen as essential to reducing the number of students who struggle in or leave school, RTI models focus on developing a strong general education, or Tier 1, program. Within Tier 1, an emphasis on curricula and instructional strategies that are backed by research can support the improved achievement of all students. This includes the use of strategies such as differentiation, universal design, and embedded literacy strategies. For many secondary schools, RTI will present a much needed vehicle through which discussions about improving the curriculum and instruction can take place. These discussions are the first step in making improvements to the instructional program. Bringing together the general education staff to discuss the horizontal (within a grade level) and vertical (across grade levels) alignment of the curriculum and to begin using common assessments to gauge the efficacy of the core instructional program can be accomplished through the use of shared leadership and the PLC framework.

The Tier 1 instructional program is accompanied by assessment procedures that help determine whether the instruction is effective. Benchmarking and screening procedures provide objective data that when coupled with other sources of information, such as attendance and engagement in school, help schools identify and target students who will likely not make sufficient progress in the curriculum without early intervention (Tier 2). When comprehensive screening processes are employed, schools can analyze and evaluate these data to determine the most effective and needed interventions based on their school populations. For example, if a screening process identifies numerous students as in need of support for reading, the school will need to investigate and adopt an intervention program for these students. Likewise, a school that experiences high absenteeism will want to consider interventions that keep students coming to school. For most secondary schools, a Tier 2 that provides a combination of academic and engagement interventions will be needed to support struggling students. Interventions should be research-based and aligned with student need.

Tier 2 will likely present the most significant change to existing school structures under an RTI framework, especially at the secondary level. Because Tier 2 can be resource intensive, it is essential to ensure that the selected interventions are effective in supporting struggling learners. Progress monitoring of student performance and growth as they receive these interventions is crucial for ensuring student success. The frequent assessment of student performance and progress allows intervention specialists to make timely and individualized adjustments and decisions. For example, if a student is not making adequate growth, the intervention specialist can make adjustments to the instruction, either by trying a different strategy, increasing the frequency or duration of the intervention lessons, or a combination of these changes. Similarly, if a student is exceeding expected growth rates, the performance target can be raised. Once students have achieved the desired performance levels and no longer need the intervention, continued monitoring of their performance in the general education program ensures that if they experience more problems, they will be "caught" and provided additional intervention.

Finally, within this system, special education (Tier 3) can move from its common, current status of a hodgepodge of intervention and support to become a focused program that provides research-based curricula for students with disabilities who require specially designed instruction. In an effective RTI system, special education is neither the placement to be avoided at all costs nor is it the catchall for any student who is difficult to teach; rather, it operates as an integral component of the system. It is aligned with general education standards but delivered through the use of specially designed instructional practices and frequent progress monitoring of growth toward individualized education goals.

WHAT IS THE ROLE OF LEADERSHIP FOR ENSURING SUCCESSFUL RTI IMPLEMENTATION?

Throughout our discussion of RTI, we have considered both the specific components necessary for RTI to work, as well as the systems-level processes that allow the components to function as an integrated system. But is a well-designed process enough to ensure that RTI delivers on the promise of leading the charge for continuous school improvement?

Strong leadership at all levels will be the key to RTI's success. Numerous authors write about the importance of effective leadership in determining the success of an education initiative. In this regard, RTI is not different than other initiatives. What is different about RTI is its comprehensive yet focused design. RTI is comprehensive in that it integrates multiple research-based practices under a single system. It is focused in that the outcome is improved outcomes for all students. That means that all actions are in place with the sole purpose of helping to improve student learning. At the secondary level, RTI has the potential to help schools build capacity for meeting the needs of all students, improve graduation rates, and lead to better teaching and learning through an integrated system. An initiative with such ambitious goals will require leadership that helps create a shared vision and empowers school personnel to be engaged in the process. In short, an ambitious initiative will require ambitious leadership at all levels.

At the national level, strong and coordinated technical assistance from centers that focus on the specific components as well as on systems-level implementation is imperative. The good news is that these centers exist and are producing many useful materials. We have identified several centers in the Resources. RTI teams should routinely consult these centers as their first stop for information. The amount of information and assistance produced and made available by technical assistance centers is growing at an exponential rate. In addition, webinars, discussion boards, and other multimedia sources of information enhance the usability of and access to this information.

At the state and district levels, policies that support RTI implementation and professional development are crucial. States that have strong guidance documents and that communicate a cohesive message about the purpose of RTI can guide implementation efforts at local levels. A good starting point for building leaders is their home state's department of education website to access any available documents and information about RTI. State and district policies should support rather than hinder schools in providing appropriate services to their students. That means providing frameworks and requirements to use evidence-based practices based on the specific needs of the building population as opposed to issuing directives to adopt one particular published curriculum. Broad, less directive policies can ensure greater success because although it is true that research-based practices are more effective than haphazard approaches to instruction, it is also true that the effects of such practices differ from population to population. Individual schools may find that some tools serve the needs of their students and fit the culture of their school better than others. If states or districts make blanket requirements to adopt a specific curriculum, it can affect the chances of successful implementation.

Finally, in recent years, almost every large-scale reform initiative has recognized strong building leadership and schoolwide buy-in as key to the reform's success. RTI is no different; strong building leadership is necessary if RTI is to be successful. RTI has numerous moving parts, requires a culture shift in the school's day-to-day operations, and presents an opportunity to integrate numerous practices to include not only what is helpful for students but also what is helpful for teachers. This cannot happen without strong leadership efforts. The building principal must understand the system, must be able to lead a needs assessment, and must develop short- and long-term goals and procedures to make implementation successful. The principal must keep staff focused on the school's goals of improved student achievement and must manage resources. The principal must lead the integration of evaluation systems that allow the school to collect, analyze, and evaluate data at the individual student level, at the classroom level, at the grade level, and at the building level—and then prioritize and act on what should happen next. RTI demands a lot from a building leader, but the reward can be significant.

As we noted in Chapter 3, an increase in the number of issues the principal is responsible for necessitates a movement toward shared leadership in schools (Portin, DeArmond, Gundlach, & Schneider, 2003). This is especially the case for secondary schools implementing RTI. Shared leadership, specifically the PLC framework, has been widely discussed as a way for principals to gain consensus among staff based on collaboration. Principals who can coordinate the strengths and passion of their staff to begin and sustain the process of RTI will be successful in their efforts. Should we be optimistic that this can happen on a large scale? Our answer is yes, and in the following section, we will explain why.

WHY WE ARE OPTIMISTIC ABOUT THE FUTURE OF RTI: TWO CASE STORIES

The leadership challenges described in the previous section may sound overwhelming. However, the school-based examples used throughout this text illustrate the possibilities for improvement when administrators tackle these challenges. In this section, we offer two case stories: (a) At the junior high level, we describe the process followed by Cheyenne Mountain Junior High School, under the leadership of this text's second author, Dr. Lori Smith, and (b) at the high school level, we describe the process implemented by Chisago Lakes High School, under the leadership of David Ertl (principal) and Sara Johnson (assistant principal).

Cheyenne Mountain Junior High

Cheyenne Mountain started its journey toward establishing an RTI model by developing a plan to meet district requirements. Although the school had been a high performing school for several years, a recent change in demographics brought an increase of students who were English language learners (at risk). The school staff were not prepared to meet the challenges of working with the at-risk population and collectively agreed that changes to their instruction and support systems would be needed to maintain their status as a high-performing school. In its first year, the school focused on putting into place interventions that would support its growing number of students whose reading ability inhibited their success in meeting the increased academic demands of the junior high. School personnel began with a simple screening mechanism, using the Diagnostic Reading Assessments (DRA) to identify students with reading levels below that of the general curriculum textbooks. Students who lagged by one or two grade levels received accommodations in the general education program; those with reading levels two grade levels or more below the reading level of their textbooks received a layered intervention— accommodations in the general education program *plus* targeted support to improve their literacy skills.

In year two, school staff recognized that although the "literacy lab" they developed during year one was effective, it would not be sufficient to fully support the needs of all students. Because the number of students struggling in their school had increased over the last few years, the traditional approaches to the general education instruction would need to change to meet the demands of their changing school population. Through the use of a PLC framework, the school formed content-area teams and charged them with investigating approaches to improving instruction, paying particular attention to differentiation, the development of common assessments, and, to the extent possible, the integration of universal design strategies. Differentiated instruction began with the use of "clickers"— technology that allows students to answer questions throughout a lesson so that teachers receive immediate feedback and can determine when they might need to provide more clarification of a particular concept.

In year three, staff continued to expand and develop their use of differentiated instruction, to include providing options for projects and assignments, as well as an increased use of multimedia to present new information. In addition, the school began to expand the availability of Tier 2 interventions to include mathematics and developed a more comprehensive system of screening. The core RTI team recognized that their current approach to screening (using grade-level reading ability) was not as effective as they would have hoped. The screening process failed to identify students who were not engaged in school. The school was already implementing a PBIS model for discipline, and Dr. Smith realized that the integration of RTI and PBIS was necessary to provide appropriate services to their struggling learners. With the guidance counselors and building leaders of the elementary schools that feed into the junior high, school staff developed a comprehensive screening tool that provided a picture of the whole child. Data from the screening tool were collected for every student, allowing the school to identify students in need of more intense interventions. The screen indicated a need for more interventions not only in academic areas but also to promote stronger study skills and to increase student engagement.

In year four, Cheyenne Mountain adopted the *Performance Series* measures in both reading and math and the AIMSweb system as a more systematic approach to progress monitoring. Through this process, the school soon realized that it needed to build a larger bank of interventions to meet the needs of students. In addition to reading and math, interventions that focused on writing, motivation, and study skills were included as a part of the Tier 2 system. In addition, the principal aligned teacher evaluations to the RTI process to emphasize the importance of a strong general education program as the foundation of the system. Teacher evaluations now include a focus on the use of differentiated instruction in the Tier 1 program and on the use of progress monitoring and effective instructional strategies for delivering the Tier 2 interventions. Evaluations are supported through collaborative planning and targeted professional development efforts.

At the time of this writing, in year five, the school has a comprehensive data-based evaluation system that has allowed all efforts to focus on ways to improve student teaching and learning. Professional development is integrated with the RTI system, and teachers requesting specific professional development must explain how it supports the school's current goals and practice before they receive authorization to attend. Accountability data are used on multiple levels from individual adjustments in instruction and intervention to review and identify school-level areas in need of attention or support. The school has maintained its status as a high-performing school, even as its student demographic has shifted dramatically over time. Student achievement in reading and writing, as measured by the Colorado state performance assessments, has increased, and discipline issues have decreased significantly. But most important, the school recognizes that continuous school improvement is a work in progress and continues to refine its RTI process.

Some of the promising outcomes achieved at Cheyenne Mountain Junior High since implementing the RTI process include a reduction in office discipline referrals from one hundred twenty-five to forty-two, a decrease from forty-six to six in the number of students who were failing courses, and maintenance of the school's high performance status despite a significant increase in the number of students who are at risk.

Chisago Lakes High School

The following case story of Chisago Lakes High School (CLHS) was provided by and developed with Sara Johnson, the assistant principal; Dave Ertl, the principal; and Holly Windram, the assistant special education director for the St. Croix River Education District (former school psychologist at CLHS). Additional descriptions and information about CLHS are provided by Windram, Scierka, and Silberglitt (2007) and Johnson, Ertl, and Windram (2009).

Chisago Lakes School District is one of five members of the St. Croix River Education District (SCRED) in Minnesota, which has a long history of implementing RTI practices (Bollman, Silberglitt, & Gibbons, 2007). CLHS consists of approximately 1,200 students in grades 9 through 12. About ten percent of their population receives special education services, eight percent receive free or reduced-priced lunch, and one percent of students are classified as ELL. CLHS has a ninety-eight percent graduation rate; but, like many secondary schools, they noted an increase in the number of incoming ninth graders with academic skill deficits, social interaction issues, and poor work completion rates. To address these concerns, they systematically began implementation of an RTI framework in the 2003–04 school year. As with Cheyenne Mountain, the RTI implementation process has evolved over the last five school years. CLHS developed their RTI model without adding any additional staff or resources, and it is entirely a general education initiative. The administrators creatively reorganized the system over time to more effectively and efficiently meet the needs of all students, particularly those in need of Tier 2 and Tier 3 supports.

In year one, CLHS, along with all SCRED schools, established a problem-solving team and process to identify students who would likely need additional support to be successful. In year two, CLHS focused on developing a toolbox of standard treatment protocol and individualized interventions, and ensuring direct observation procedures were built into the system to ensure implementation integrity of both instruction and progress monitoring at Tier 2 and Tier 3. In year three, an RTI English 9 class was built into the master schedule as a standard treatment protocol for students who required an additional focus on literacy skill development. The class is designed around research-based practices in literacy instruction for secondary students (e.g., Alliance for Excellence in Education, 2004; Diamond, 2004), including formative progress monitoring Curriculum-based Measurement (CBM) oral reading fluency (ORF) and correct writing sequences (CWS). In year four, an RTI English 10 class was developed for students who were making progress but still required additional Tier 2 support. In addition, the school adopted a "Check and Connect" intervention program (Christenson et al., 2008) designed in partnership with Dr. Sandra Christenson from the University of Minnesota to address issues with student engagement. In year five, CLHS continued to refine its use of DBDM for students receiving Tier 2 or Tier 3 supports and began focusing on interventions for math. In year six, CLHS continues to refine the application of a five-step problem-solving process with integrity across all tiers and to expand the toolbox of intervention options for secondary students.

The following description of the process reflects CLHS's current model of RTI. CLHS currently uses a four-tiered model of RTI, in which Tier 1 represents the general education program; Tier 2 represents intervention provided through a standard treatment protocol approach; Tier 3 represents a more intense level of interventions, provided in small groups or 1:1; and Tier 4 represents special education. At the heart of the RTI framework at CLHS—as well as all other SCRED schools—is instructional decision making using a five-step problem-solving model (Batsche & Knoff, 1995; Knoff, 2002) that is data-driven (Bollman, Silberglitt, & Gibbons, 2007).

The problem-solving team is facilitated by the assistant principal and includes guidance counselors, the school psychologist, the school nurse, a police liaison officer, truancy prevention representative, and a mental health representative. The problem-solving team uses a five-step problem-solving model:

1. Problem identification

2. Problem analysis

3. Plan development

4. Plan implementation

5. Plan evaluation

Each Monday the problem-solving team meets to review student referrals to the team by teachers, counselors, or parents. The team ensures problem identification data are collected and decides the degree of intervention intensity needed to address the problem that is prioritized. Less intensive intervention includes consultation with other teachers or student support services (e.g., the school psychologist or school counselor) to address the problem. Secondarily, the student may be assigned to a standard treatment protocol intervention (Tier 2). If the concern is severe enough, a subgroup of problem-solving team members will meet at a separate time to conduct more formal problem analysis (e.g., curriculum-based evaluation or a functional behavior assessment), and develop a more individualized intervention plan (Tier 3). This meeting is facilitated by the school psychologist. Data are systematically reviewed by a team using the problem-solving process. Data reviews are facilitated by the school psychologist. Progress monitoring data are reviewed one time per month by the problem-solving team for all students receiving a Tier 3 intervention. Data for students receiving a standard treatment protocol intervention are also reviewed two times per quarter by teachers, the school psychologist, guidance counselors, and the assistant principal.

In the spring of each year, multiple data sources used for the incoming ninth graders are reviewed to determine placement for standard treatment protocol interventions for fall of ninth grade. These data sources include the following:

- CBM scores on ORF, CWS, and Math Applications
- Performance on the Measures of Academic Progress (MAP)
- Performance on state level tests
- Attendance and grades
- Current eighth-grade class enrollment

- Current information from the middle school problem-solving team
- Eighth-grade teacher input and recommendation

For example, students who are identified through this process as in need of targeted intervention in literacy are placed in the RTI English 9 class. For the first quarter of the school year, goals of the RTI English 9 class are to (a) build relationships with students, (b) establish a regular cycle of CBM data collection and review, and (c) begin problem solving on students who are not making progress within the first four to five weeks of school. The RTI English classes are held daily for one eighty-five-minute block all year. Students in the RTI English class receive double the instructional time or reading and writing interventions and a modified core English curriculum. The classes are cotaught by an English teacher and intervention specialists.

During the first quarter, the RTI English 9 class includes whole-group academic interventions for reading fluency and writing mechanics. Instructional strategies such as peer tutoring and repeated readings are used to develop these skills. At the end of the first quarter, additional needs of the students are identified, and supplemental instruction is adapted for students who require supports not addressed by the standard-treatment protocols used for fluency and writing. These decisions are made based on performance on CBM in ORF and CWS as well as performance on MAP assessments. CBM reading and writing data are collected on every student, and data reviews are conducted twice each quarter. SCRED has established target scores for these measures, and student performance and growth are compared with these targets to determine if students are responding to the intervention. In the 2005–06 school year, more than seventy percent of students in the RTI English 9 class met their individual growth targets. Next steps for the 2009–10 school year include building greater capacity in the area of math and expanding the CLHS Check and Connect program to include more students. Since beginning the process of RTI implementation, CLHS has seen a reduction in the failure rate of ninth-grade students from twenty-three percent to ten percent. The school continues to refine the RTI process through a sustained integration of instruction, intervention, assessment, documentation of implementation integrity, and professional development.

Textbox 8.1 Lessons Learned Regarding RTI Implementation

1. Focus on leader requirements to develop the system.

2. Commit to a multiple-year process of implementation.

3. Program evaluation and DBDM are critical components of the RTI process.

4. Improved student outcomes are the bottom line of implementation.

SUMMARY

The case stories presented in this chapter provide promising rationales for moving forward with RTI implementation at the secondary level. Though each school will look different as it begins the process of RTI implementation, some of the big lessons learned at Cheyenne Mountain Junior High and Chisago Lakes High School can guide other schools as they move forward with RTI (see Textbox 8.1, "Lessons Learned Regarding RTI Implementation," on page 124). First, RTI is not just a bunch of components implemented in a disjointed fashion. A school can implement the individual components, but if it lacks the vision and the integrated system that make the RTI process work, its efforts will not be successful. This can be avoided if there is a strong focus on leader responsibilities in addition to the specifics of the process. Second, both schools' journey of implementation has reached year five, and they are not done yet. The staff recognizes that continuous school improvement is just that—continuous. Schools undertaking this process must commit to a multiple-year reform effort. Third, program evaluation and the use of data for continuous school improvement are ideas whose time have come—they are *critical* components of the RTI process and must be used effectively if the system is to work. Data-based Decision Making is not a new concept, but it has gained new attention through accountability requirements and the focus on integrated assessment and instructional systems. RTI cannot be successful without a strong DBDM system. Finally, maintaining and reviewing data on student outcomes are necessary parts of the RTI process. Without the collection and review of such data, a school will not know if its efforts are successful.

Cheyenne Mountain and Chisago Lakes are just two of many success stories about RTI. Our hope is that through this text, we have provided you with helpful information and resources that will enable you to begin your own school's success story.

Appendix

RTI Implementation Checklist

ESSENTIAL TASK LIST FOR SCREENING

Directions: In the second column, *Responsible Person(s)*, write the name(s) of the individual or team who will assume responsibility for the task identified in the first column. In the third column, *Timeline/Status*, write the deadline for the task and/or the status of the task.

Task	Responsible Person(s)	Timeline/Status
Review your screening instrument's items to be certain that content is aligned with the curriculum for each grade level.		
Once a tool has been selected, determine and secure the resources required for implementation (e.g., computers, folders and copies, testing areas).		
Determine initial professional development needs and ongoing training support.		
Administer the screening measure three times a year (early fall, midterm, and late spring).		
Create a database that aligns with the screening instrument to hold student information and scores.		
Organize the screening results (e.g., graphs and tables) to provide a profile of all students and comparisons with each other.		
Monitor results at the classroom level and make decisions about when teachers or instructional programs require more scrutiny and support.		
Add screening results to a database so that students' performance can be monitored over time.		
Specify written steps to follow when further scrutiny is needed for students judged to be at risk.		

Mellard, D. F., & Johnson, E. (2008). *RTI: A practitioner's guide to implementing response to intervention*. Thousand Oaks, CA: Corwin. Used with permission.

Resources

The following resources provide more information about key ideas presented in this text.

All Things PLC: http://www.allthingsplc.info

This website, developed by Solution Tree, provides commercial-free information and resources for teachers and administrators interested in implementing the PLC framework to improve student achievement.

Center for Applied Special Technology: http://www.cast.org

This center's mission is to provide information and technical assistance related to Universal Design for Learning (UDL). UDL offers one way through which teachers can differentiate instruction through the use of technology. In addition to research and publications, this website includes numerous helpful planning tools and lesson-plan ideas for teachers across content areas.

Center for Research on Learning: http://www.kucrl.org

The Center for Research on Learning at the University of Kansas has conducted research and developed a model of strategic instruction, the Strategic Instructional Model, for teachers to use to help adolescents with learning disabilities and who are at risk become independent learners and critical thinkers.

Center on Instruction: http://www.centeroninstruction.org

The Center on Instruction is a partnership of five organizations that provides expertise to the Regional Comprehensive Centers in reading, math, special education, and English language learners. The website includes resources and information in each of these areas, with a focus on progress monitoring and assessment.

Data-based Decision-Making Resources for Educators: http://www.ael.org/dbdm

This website is a joint project between Edvantia, an education research and development corporation, and the Council of Chief State School Officers; it provides information and resources to school-based teams on the use of DBDM to improve student outcomes.

Intervention Central: http://www.interventioncentral.org

This site offers free tools and resources to help school staff and parents to promote positive classroom behaviors and foster effective learning for all students. The site was created by Jim Wright, a school psychologist from Syracuse, New York.

Kansas Coaching Project, Instructional Coaching: http://www.instructionalcoach.org

Developed by Jim Knight at the University of Kansas Center for Research on Learning, this website is dedicated to information on instructional coaching. Resources on this site include general information about instructional coaching, tools for coaches, and opportunities for training.

National Association for Secondary School Principals (NASSP) Breaking Ranks: http://www.nassp.org

The Breaking Ranks model of school reform focuses on the central issue of student performance. Numerous materials such as surveys, professional development workshops, and online assessment tools are detailed on the National Association for Secondary School Principals website.

National Center for Learning Disabilities RTI Action Network: http://www.rtinetwork.org

The RTI Action Network is a program of the National Center for Learning Disabilities and provides technical assistance and information about RTI. Included on the site are articles, examples, and links to other resources to support the effective implementation of RTI.

National Center on Response to Intervention: http://www.rti4success.org

The National Center on RTI is funded by the U.S. Department of Education's Office of Special Education Programs with the mission of providing technical assistance to states and districts and building the capacity of states to assist districts in implementing proven models for RTI.

National Center on Student Progress Monitoring: http://www.studentprogress.org

The center's mission is to provide technical assistance to states and districts and to disseminate information about progress-monitoring practices proven to work in different academic content areas.

National High School Center: http://www.betterhighschools.org

This center provides information on the use of its "Early Warning System" to collect and analyze data related to attendance, behavior, and academic performance that are strong predictors of high school completion.

National Middle School Association: http://www.nmsa.org

The National Middle School Association is a national education association dedicated exclusively to students in the middle grades. The website includes extensive information on school improvement at the middle grade levels, to include self-assessment kits and access to professional development opportunities.

National Staff Development Council: http://www.nsdc.org

The National Staff Development Council's purpose is ensuring that every educator engages in effective professional learning every day so every student achieves. It includes resources for staff development and whole-school improvement models.

National Technical Assistance Center on Positive Behavioral Interventions & Supports: http://www.pbis.org

The National Technical Assistance Center on Positive Behavioral Interventions & Supports is funded by the U.S. Office of Special Education Programs with the mission of providing technical assistance on the behavioral and discipline systems needed for successful learning and social development of students. The Center provides information and technical support about behavioral systems to assist states and districts.

Project AAIMS: http://www.ci.hs.iastate.edu/ aaims/resources.php

Project Algebra Assessment and Instruction—Meeting Standards (AAIMS) was designed to achieve two objectives related to the teaching and learning of algebra for students with and without disabilities. Information on instructional techniques and progress monitoring tools is available on this website.

Research Institute on Progress Monitoring: http://www.progressmonitoring.net

The institute's mission is to develop a system of progress monitoring to evaluate the effects of individualized instruction on access to and progress within the general education curriculum. The Research Institute on Progress Monitoring researches ways to monitor student progress and has led the development of progress monitoring procedures, especially at the secondary level.

SEDL: http://www.sedl.org

SEDL is a private, nonprofit education research, development, and dissemination corporation based in Austin, Texas. Its website includes information on the school change process and leadership.

State Implementation and Scaling-Up of Evidence-based Practices: http://www.fpg.unc.edu/~sisep/about-us.cfm

The purpose of the State Implementation and Scaling-Up of Evidence-based Practices center is to promote students' academic achievement and behavioral health by supporting implementation and scaling-up of evidence-based practices in education settings. One of the center's goals is to define a conceptual framework and logic model for sustained, large-scale implementation of evidence-based practices in education.

The Wallace Foundation: http://www.wallacefoundation.org

The Wallace Foundation is a private organization that provides grants, research, and related activities to support and share effective ideas and practices that strengthen education leadership.

References

Allen, J. (2004). *Tools for teaching content literacy.* Portland, ME: Stenhouse Publishers.

Alliance for Excellence in Education. (2004). *Reading next: A vision for action and research in middle and high school literacy.* Washington, DC: Author.

American Association of School Administrators. (2002). *Using data to improve schools: What's working.* Arlington, VA: KSA-Plus Communications. Retrieved July 5, 2009, from http://aasa.files.cmsplus.com/PDFs/Publications/Using DataToImproveSchools.pdf

Archer, A., Gleason, M. M., & Vachon, V. (2000). *Rewards secondary.* Frederick, CO: Sopris West.

Ascher, C., Henderson, A. T., & Maguire, C. (2008). *Putting kids on the pathway to college: How is your school doing?* Providence, RI: Annenberg Institute for School Reform, Brown University.

Balfanz, R., Herzog, L., & Mac Iver, D. J. (2007). Preventing student disengagement and keeping students on the graduation path in urban middle-grades schools: Early identification and effective interventions. *Educational Psychologist, 42*(4), 223–235.

Batsche, G. M., & Knoff, H. M. (1995). Best practices in linking assessment to intervention. In A. Thomes & J. Grimes (Eds.), *Best practices in school psychology* (3rd ed., pp. 569–586). Bethesda, MD: National Association of School Psychologists.

Berglund, R., & Johns, J. (2002). *Strategies for content area learning: Vocabulary, comprehension, and response.* Dubuque, IA: Kendall-Hunt Publishing Co.

Biancarosa, G., & Snow, C. (2004). *Reading next: A vision for action and research in middle and high school literacy.* Washington, DC: Alliance for Excellent Education.

Bollman, K. A., Silberglitt, B, & Gibbons, K. A. (2007). The St. Croix River Education District model: Incorporating systems-level organization and a multi-tiered problem-solving process for intervention delivery. In S. Jimerson, M. Burns, & A. VanDerHayden (Eds.), *Handbook of Response to Intervention: The science and practice of assessment and intervention* (pp. 244–251). New York: Springer.

Bridgeland, J. M., DiIulio, J. J., & Morison, K. B. (2006). *The silent epidemic: Perspectives of high school dropouts.* Washington, DC: Civic Enterprises and Peter D. Hart Research Associates.

Busch, T., & Espin, C. A. (2003). Using curriculum-based measurement to prevent failure and assess learning in content areas. *Assessment for Effective Intervention, 28,* 49–58.

Cash, M. M., & Schumm, J. S. (2006). Making sense of knowledge: Comprehending expository text. In J. Schumm (Ed.), *Reading assessment and instruction for all learners* (pp. 262–296). New York: Guilford Press.

Center on Education Policy. (2008). *State high school exit exams: A move toward end-of-course exams.* Washington, DC: Author.

Christenson, S. L., Thurlow, M. L., Sinclair, M. F., Lehr, C. A., Kaibel, C. M., Reschly, et al. (2008). *Check & Connect: A comprehensive student engagement intervention manual* Minneapolis: Institute on Community Integration, University of Minnesota.

Compton, D. L., Fuchs, D., Fuchs, L. S., & Bryant, J. D. (2006). Selecting at-risk readers in first grade for early intervention: A two-year longitudinal study of decision rules and procedures. *Journal of Educational Psychology, 98,* 394–409.

Conley, M. (2008). Cognitive strategy instruction for adolescents: What we know about the promise, what we don't know about the potential. *Harvard Educational Review, 78*(1), 84–106.

Covey, S. R. (2004). *The 7 habits of highly effective people.* Roseburg, OR: Free Press.

Deno, S. L. (1985). Curriculum-based measurement: The emerging alternative. *Exceptional Children, 52,* 219–232.

Deno, S. L. (2001). *Curriculum-based measures: Development and perspectives.* Minneapolis: University of Minnesota, Research Institute on Progress Monitoring.

Deno, S. L., & Mirkin, P. K. (1977). *Data-based program modification: A manual.* Reston, VA: Council for Exceptional Children.

Deshler, D., & Mellard, D. F. (2006, April). *RTI and Scaling Up.* Presented at the Council for Exceptional Children DLD conference. Retrieved July 5, 2009, from www.nrcld.org/about/presentations/2006/DeshlerScalingUpCEC2006 .pdf

Deshler, D., Palinscar, A., Biancarosa, G., & Nair, M. (2007). *Informed choices for struggling adolescent readers: A research-based guide to instructional programs and practices.* New York: Carnegie Corporation.

Deshler, D. D., Schumaker, J. B., Lenz, K. B., Bulgren, J. A., Hock, M. F., Knight, J., et al. (2009). Ensuring content-area learning by secondary students with learning disabilities. In T. Skrtic, E. Horn, & G. Clark (Eds.), *Taking stock of special education policy & practice: A retrospective commentary* (pp. 30–49). Denver, CO: Love Publishing.

Diamond, L. (2004). *Implementing and sustaining a middle and high school reading intervention program.* Berkeley, CA: The Consortium on Reading Excellence, Inc.

Dolejs, C. (2006). *Report on key practices and policies of consistently higher performing effective schools.* Washington, DC: National High School Center, U.S. Department of Education. Retrieved July 5, 2009, from http://www.betterhighschools .org/topics/HighSchoolReform.asp

Duffy, H. (2007). *Meeting the needs of significantly struggling learners in high school: A look at approaches to tiered intervention.* Washington, DC: National High School Center.

DuFour, R., & Eaker, R. E. (1998). *Professional Learning Communities at work: Best practices for enhancing student achievement.* Bloomington, IN: National Education Service.

DuFour, R., DuFour, R., Eaker, R., & Many, T. (2006). *Learning by doing: A handbook for Professional Learning Communities at work.* Bloomington, IN: Solution Tree.

Education Commission of the States. (2006). *Standard high school graduation requirements (50-state)*. Washington, DC: Author. Retrieved July 5, 2009, from http://nces.ed.gov/programs/coe/2007/analysis/sa_table.asp?tableID=851

Elmore, R. (2007). *Educational improvement in Victoria*. Victoria, Canada: Office of Government, School, Education, Department of Education. Retrieved July 5, 2009, from http://www.eduweb.vic.gov.au/edulibrary/public/staffdev/schlead/Richard_Elmore-wps-v1–20070817.pdf

Espin, C. A., Busch, T., Shin, J., & Kruschwitz, R. (2001). Curriculum-based measures in the content areas: Validity of vocabulary-matching measures as indicators of performance in social studies. *Learning Disabilities Research and Practice, 16,* 142–151.

Espin, C. A., & Foegen, A. (1996). Validity of three general outcome measures for predicting secondary students' performance on content-area tasks. *Exceptional Children, 62,* 497–514.

Espin, C. A., Skare, S., Shin, J., Deno, S. L., Robinson, S., & Brenner, B. (2000). Identifying indicators of growth in written expression for middle-school students. *Journal of Special Education, 34,* 140–153.

Espin, C. A., & Tindal, G. (1999). The use of curriculum-based measurement for secondary students. In M. R. Shinn (Ed.), *Advanced applications of curriculum-based measurement* (pp. 214–253). New York: Guildford Press.

Fisher, D., & Johnson, C. (2006). Analyzing student work. *Principal Leadership, 7,* 27–31.

Fletcher, J. M., Lyon, G. R., Fuchs, L. S., & Barnes, M. A. (2007). *Learning disabilities: From identification to intervention*. New York: Guilford Press.

Flannery, K. B., Sugai, G., Eber, L., & Bohanon-Edmondson, H. (Eds.). (2004). *Positive behavior support in high schools: Monograph from the 2004 Illinois high school forum of positive behavior interventions and supports*. Retrieved July 5, 2009, from http://www.pbis.org/pbis_resource_detail_page.aspx?Type=3&PBIS_ResourceID=271

Foegen, A., Olson, J. R., & Impecoven-Lind, L. (2008). Developing progress monitoring measures for secondary mathematics. *Assessment for Effective Intervention, 33*(4), 240–249.

Fuchs, D., & Deshler, D. D. (2007). What we need to know about responsiveness-to-intervention (and shouldn't be afraid to ask). *Learning Disabilities Research and Practice, 22*(2), 129–136.

Fuchs, D., Mock, D., Morgan, P. L., & Young, C. L. (2003). Responsiveness-to-intervention: Definitions, evidence, and implications for the learning disabilities construct. *Learning Disabilities Research and Practice, 18*(3), 157–171.

Fuchs, L. S. (2007). *Monitoring student progress in the classroom to enhance teacher planning and student learning*. Webinar presented by the National Center on Student Progress Monitoring. Retrieved July 5, 2009, from http://www.studentprogress.org

Fuchs, L. S., & Deno, S. L. (1991). Paradigmatic distinctions between instructionally relevant measurement models. *Exceptional Children, 57,* 488–501.

Fuchs, L. S., Deno, S. L., & Mirkin, P. K. (1984). The effects of frequent curriculum-based measurement and evaluation on pedagogy, student achievement, and student awareness of learning. *American Educational Research Journal, 21,* 449–460.

Fuchs, L. S., & Fuchs, D. (2006). Implementing responsiveness-to-intervention to identify learning disabilities. *Perspectives on Dyslexia, 32,* 1, 39–43.

Fullan, M. (2001). *The new meaning of educational change* (3rd ed.). New York: Teachers College Press.

Fullan, M. (2004). *Leadership and sustainability: System thinkers in action.* Thousand Oaks, CA: Corwin.

Gersten, R., Chard, D., & Baker, S. (2000). Factors enhancing sustained use of research-based instructional practices. *Journal of Learning Disabilities, 33*(5), 445–457.

Gickling, E. E., & Havertape, S. (1981). *Curriculum-based assessment.* Minneapolis, MN: School Psychology Inservice Training Network.

Goe, L. (2006). *The teacher preparation—teacher practices—student outcomes relationship in special education: Missing links and next steps. A research synthesis.* Washington, DC: National Comprehensive Center for Teacher Quality.

Goodlad, J. I., Mantle-Bromley, C., & Goodlad, S. J. (2004). *Education for everyone: Agenda for education in a democracy,* San Francisco: Jossey-Bass.

Graham, S., & Perin, D. (2007). *Writing next: Effective strategies to improve writing of adolescents in middle and high schools: A report to Carnegie Corporation of New York.* Washington, DC: Alliance for Excellent Education.

Hakim, J. (1999). *A history of us: War, terrible war, 1860–1865, Book 6.* New York: Oxford University Press.

Heifetz, R. L., & Linsky, M. (2002). *Leadership on the line: Staying alive through the dangers of leading.* Boston: Harvard Business School Publishing.

Heppen, J. B., & Therriault, S. B. (2008). *Developing early warning systems to identify potential high school dropouts.* Washington, DC: National High School Center.

Hill, P. T., & Celio, M. B. (1998). *Fixing urban schools.* Washington, DC: Brookings Institution Press.

Hintze, J. M., & Silberglitt, B. (2005). A longitudinal examination of the diagnostic accuracy and predictive validity of R-CBM and high stakes testing. *School Psychology Review, 34*(3), 372–386.

Hock, M., Schumaker, J. B., & Deshler, D. D. (2001). *Possible selves: Nurturing student motivation.* Lawrence, KS: Edge Enterprises.

Honig, M. I., & Hatch, T. C. (2004). Policy coherence: How schools strategically manage multiple, external demands. *Educational Researcher, 33*(8), 16–30.

Hosp, M., Hosp, J., & Howell, K. (2007). *The ABCs of CBM.* New York: Guilford Press.

Individuals with Disabilities Education Act of 2004. (2004). Public Law 108–446.

Jenkins, J. R., & Johnson, E. S. (2008). *Universal screening for reading problems: Why and how should we do this?* Washington, DC: RTI Action Network, National Center for Learning Disabilities. Retrieved July 5, 2009, from http://www.rtinetwork.org/Essential/Assessment/Universal/ar/ReadingProblems

Jerald, C. D. (2006). *Identifying potential dropouts: Key lessons for building an early warning data system.* Washington, DC: Achieve, Inc.

Jerald, C. D. (2007). *Keeping kids in school: What research says about preventing dropouts.* Washington, DC: Center for Public Education.

Johnson, E. S., Greenlee, R., & Brown, D. (2009). *Monitoring student progress in science with a vocabulary matching measure.* Manuscript in preparation.

Johnson, E. S., Jenkins, J. R., Petscher, Y., & Catts, H. W. (2009). How can we improve the accuracy of screening instruments? *Learning Disabilities Research and Practice, 24,* 3.

Johnson, E., & Mellard, D. F. (2006). *Getting started with SLD determination: After IDEA reauthorization.* Lawrence, KS: National Research Center on Learning Disabilities.

Johnson, E. S., & Smith, L. (2008). Implementing Response to Intervention in middle school: Challenges and potential benefits. *Teaching Exceptional Children, 40*(3), 46–52.

Johnson, S., Ertl, D., & Windram, H. (2009). *Successful implementation of RTI at the secondary level: Strategies and solutions learned.* Presentation given at the Minnesota RTI Center Conference: Quality Literacy Instruction and Systems That Support It, St. Croix, MN.

Kamil, M. L., Borman, G. D., Dole, J., Kral, C. C., Salinger, T., & Torgesen, J. (2008). *Improving adolescent literacy: Effective classroom and intervention practices: A Practice Guide* (NCEE #2008–4027). Washington, DC: National Center for Education Evaluation and Regional Assistance, Institute of Education Sciences, U.S. Department of Education. Retrieved July 5, 2009, from http:// ies.ed.gov/ncee/wwc/pdf/practiceguides/adlit_pg_082608.pdf

Kennelly, L., & Monrad, M. (2007). *Approaches to dropout prevention: Heeding early warning signs with appropriate interventions.* Washington, DC: National High School Center, American Institutes for Research.

Klingner, J. K., Vaughn, S., & Schumm, J. D. (1998). Collaborative strategic reading in heterogeneous classrooms. *Elementary School Journal, 99,* 3–21.

Knoff, H. M. (2002). Best practices in facilitating school reform, organizational change, and strategic planning. In A. Thomas & J. Grimes (Eds.), *Best practices in school psychology* (4th ed., pp. 235–253). Bethesda, MD: National Association of School Psychologists.

Kovaleski, J. F. (2003, December). *The three tier model for identifying learning disabilities: Critical program features and system issues.* Paper presented at the National Research Center on Learning Disabilities Responsiveness-to-Intervention symposium, Kansas City, MO.

Lachat, M. A. (2001). *Data-driven high school reform: Breaking ranks model.* Providence, RI: Northeast and Islands Regional Educational Laboratory.

Langer, J. A. (2001). Beating the odds: Teaching middle and high school students to read and write well. *American Educational Research Journal, 38,* 837–880.

Lashway, L. (2003). Distributed leadership. *Research Roundup, 19,* 4. Eugene, OR: ERIC Clearinghouse on Educational Management.

Lembke, E., & Stecker, P. (2007). *Curriculum-based measurement in mathematics: An evidence-based formative assessment procedure.* Portsmouth, NH: RMC Research Corporation, Center on Instruction.

Marston, D., Muyskens, P., Lau, M., & Canter, A. (2003). Problem-solving model for decision making with high-incidence disabilities: The Minneapolis experience. *Learning Disabilities Research & Practice, 18*(3), 187–200.

Marzano, R. (2003). *What works in schools.* Alexandria, VA: ASCD.

McMaster, K., Fuchs, D., Fuchs, L. S., & Compton, D. L. (2003, December). *Responding to non-responders: An experimental field trial of identification and intervention methods.* Paper presented at the National Research Center on Learning Disabilities Responsiveness-to-Intervention Symposium, Kansas City, MO.

McTighe, J., & Emberger, M. (2006). Teamwork on assessments creates powerful professional development. *Journal of Staff Development, 27,* 1, 38–44.

Mellard, D. F., Byrd, S. E., Johnson, E., Tollefson, J. M., & Boesche, L. (2004). Foundations and research on identifying model responsiveness-to-intervention sites. *Learning Disability Quarterly, 27,* 243–256.

Mellard, D. F., & Johnson, E. S. (2008). *RTI: A practitioner's guide to implementing Response to Intervention.* Thousand Oaks, CA: Corwin.

National Association of Secondary School Principals. (1996). Breaking ranks: Changing an American institution. *NASSP Bulletin, 80*(578), 55–66.

National Middle School Association. (2003). *This we believe: Successful schools for young adolescents.* Westerville, OH: National Middle School Association.

National Technical Assistance Center on Positive Behavioral Interventions & Supports. (n.d.). *What is school-wide PBS?* Retrieved July 5, 2009, from http:// www.pbis.org/schoolwide.htm#StepsInvolved

No Child Left Behind (NCLB) Act. (2001). Public Law 107–110.

Nunley, K. F. (2006). *Differentiating the high school classroom: Solution strategies for 18 common obstacles.* Thousand Oaks, CA: Corwin.

Ogle, D. M. (1986). K-W-L: A teaching model that develops active reading of expository text. *The Reading Teacher, 39*(6), 564–570.

Palinscar, A. (1984). The quest for meaning from expository text: A teacher guided journey. In G. Duffy, L. Roehler, & J. Mason (Eds.), *Comprehension instruction: Perspectives and suggestions* (pp. 251–264). New York: Longman.

Palinscar, A., & Brown , R. (1984). Reciprocal teaching of comprehension-fostering and monitoring activities. *Cognition and Instruction, 1*(2), 117–175.

Portin, B. S., DeArmond, M., Gundlach, L., & Schneider, P. (2003). *Making sense of leading schools: A national study of the principalship.* Seattle: University of Washington, Center on Reinventing Public Education.

Pressley, M. (2000). What should comprehension instruction be the instruction of? In M. Kamil, P. Mosenthal, P. Pearson, & R. Barr (Eds.), *Handbook of reading research* (Vol. III, pp. 545–561). Mahwah, NJ: Erlbaum.

Pressley, M., El-Dinary, P., Gaskins, I., Schuder, T., Bergman, J. L., Almasi, J., et al. (1992). Beyond direct explanation: Transactional instruction of reading comprehension strategies. *The Elementary School Journal, 92*(5), 513–555.

Pressley, M., & Hilden, K. (2004). Cognitive strategies: Production deficiencies and successful strategy instruction everywhere, In D. Kuhn & R. Seigler (Eds.), *Handbook of child psychology* (Vol. 2, pp. 400–480). Hoboken, NJ: Wiley & Sons.

Raphael, T. E. (1986). Teaching question-answer relationships, revisited. *The Reading Teacher, 39,* 516–523.

Reeves, D. B. (2002, March/April). Accountability-based reforms should lead to better teaching and learning-period. *Harvard Education Letter.* Retrieved July 5, 2009, from http://www.edletter.org/past/issues/2002-ma/reeves.shtml

Reid, W. A. (1987). Institutions and practices: Professional education reports and the language of reform. *Educational Researcher, 16*(8), 10–15.

Reid, W. A. (2007). Practical reasoning and curriculum theory: In search of a new paradigm. *Curriculum Inquiry, 9*(3), 187–207.

Research Institute on Progress Monitoring. (n.d.). *Resources: Curriculum-based measurement at the secondary-school level.* Minneapolis: University of Minnesota. Retrieved July 5, 2009, from http://www.progressmonitoring.net/RIPM Products2.html#cbm_secondary

Salvia, J., Ysseldyke, J., & Bolt, S. (2006). *Assessment in special and inclusive education* (10th ed.). Florence, KY: Wadsworth Publishing Company.

Sandomierski, T., Kincaid, D., & Algozzine, B. (2007). Response to Intervention and positive behavior support: brothers from different mothers or sisters with different misters? *PBIS Newsletter, 4*(2). Retrieved July 5, 2009, from http:// www.pbis.org/pbis_newsletter/volume_4/default.aspx

Scantron®, a registered trademark of the Scantron Corporation.

Schweinhart, L. J. (2004). *The HighScope Perry preschool study through age 40: Summary, conclusions, and frequently asked questions.* Ypsilanti, MI: HighScope Press.

Shapiro, E. (2004). *Academic skills problems: Direct assessment and intervention* (3rd ed.). New York: Guilford Press.

Shinn, M. (2005). *Administration and scoring of written expression curriculum-based measurement (WE-CBM).* Eden Prairie, MN: Edformation. Retrieved July 5, 2009, from http://www.aimsweb.com

Snow, C., Porche, M. V., Tabors, P. O., & Harris, S. R. (2007). *Is literacy enough? Pathways to academic success for adolescents.* Baltimore: Brookes Publishing.

Spillane, J. P., Reiser, B. J., & Reimer, T. (2002). Policy implementation and cognition: Reframing and refocusing implementation research. *Review of Educational Research, 72,* 387–431.

Stanovich, K. E. (1986). Matthew effects in reading: Some consequences of individual differences in the acquisition of literacy. *Reading Research Quarterly, 21,* 360–407.

StatSoft, Inc. (2007). *Electronic statistics textbook.* Tulsa, OK: StatSoft. Retrieved July 5, 2009, from http://www.statsoft.com/textbook/stathome.html

Stecker, P. M., Fuchs, L. S., & Fuchs, D. (2005). Using curriculum-based measurement to improve student achievement: Review of research. *Psychology in the Schools, 42,* 795–819.

Stecker, P. M., & Lembke, E. S. (2005). *Advanced applications of CBM in reading: Instructional decision-making strategies manual.* Washington, DC: National Center on Student Progress Monitoring. Retrieved July 5, 2009, from http://www.studentprogress.org

Stein, M., Kinder, D., Silbert, J., & Carnine, D. W. (2006). *Designing effective mathematics instruction: A direct instruction approach* (4th ed.). Upper Saddle River, NJ: Prentice Hall.

Stiggins, R. (2002, June). Assessment crisis: The absence of assessment for learning. *Phi Delta Kappan, 83*(10), 758–765.

Sugai, G. (2007, December). *Responsiveness-to-intervention: Lessons learned and to be learned.* Keynote presentation at and paper for the RTI Summit, U.S. Department of Education, Washington, DC.

Sugai, G., Flannery, K. B., & Bohanon-Edmonson, H. (2004). *Positive behavior support in high schools: Monograph from the 2004 Illinois high school forum of positive behavioral interventions and supports,* unpublished manuscript, University of Oregon, Eugene.

Sugai, G., & Horner, R. H. (1999). Discipline and behavioral support: Preferred processes and practices. *Effective School Practices, 17*(4), 10–22.

Sugai, G., & Horner, R. H. (2002). The evolution of discipline practices: School-wide positive behavior supports. *Child and Family Behavior Therapy, 24,* 23–50.

Swanson, H. L., & Deshler, D. (2003). Instructing adolescents with learning disabilities: Converting a meta-analysis to practice. *Journal of Learning Disabilities, 36*2), 124–135.

Tomlinson, C. A. (2001). *How to differentiate instruction in mixed-ability classrooms* (2nd ed.). Alexandria, VA: ASCD.

Torgesen, J. K., Houston, D. D., Rissman, L. M., Decker, S. M., Roberts, G., Vaughn, S., et al. (2007). *Academic literacy instruction for adolescents: A guidance document from the Center on Instruction.* Portsmouth, NH: RMC Research Corporation, Center on Instruction.

U.S. Department of Education. (2002). *Strategies for making adequate yearly progress, using curriculum-based measurement for progress monitoring.* Presentation given at the Student Achievement and School Accountability Conference. Retrieved July 5, 2009, from http://www.ed.gov/admins/lead/account/aypstr/edlite-index.html

Vaughn, S. (2003, December). *How many tiers are needed for Response to Intervention to achieve acceptable prevention outcomes?* Paper presented at the NRCLD Responsiveness to Intervention Symposium, Kansas City, MO. Retrieved July 5, 2009, from http://www.nrcld.org/symposium2003/vaughn/index.html

Vaughn, S., Speece, D., & Linan-Thompson, S. (2008). *Response to Intervention in reading at the middle grades.* Presentation given at the Pacific Coast Regional Conference, Coronado, CA.

Wayman, J. C., Stringfield, S. & Yakimowski, M. (2004). *Software enabling school improvement through analysis of student data* [Report No. 67]. Baltimore: Johns Hopkins University, Center for Research on the Education of Students Placed at Risk. Retrieved July 5, 2009, from http://www.csos.jhu.edu

Wedman, J. (2007). *The performance pyramid: Needs assessment made simple.* Columbia: University of Missouri. Retrieved July 5, 2009, from http://needs assessment.missouri.edu/resources.php

Wiggins, G., & McTighe, J. (2007). *Schooling by design: Mission, action and achievement.* Alexandria, VA: Association of Supervision and Curriculum Development.

Windram, H., Scierka, B., & Silberglitt, B. (2007). Response to Intervention at the secondary level: Two districts' models of implementation. *Communiqué, 35*(5), 43–45

Worthen, B. R., Sanders, J. R., & Fitzpatrick, J. L. (1997). *Program evaluation: Alternative approaches and practical guidelines* (2nd ed.). White Plains, NY: Addison-Wesley.

Zieky, M., & Perie, M. (2006). *A primer on setting cut scores on tests of educational achievement.* Princeton, NJ: Educational Testing Services.

Index

CORWIN

A SAGE Company

The Corwin logo—a raven striding across an open book—represents the union of courage and learning. Corwin is committed to improving education for all learners by publishing books and other professional development resources for those serving the field of PreK–12 education. By providing practical, hands-on materials, Corwin continues to carry out the promise of its motto: **"Helping Educators Do Their Work Better."**